Praise for
DO IT! SPEAKING

"Few people have their pulse on the speaking industry better than David Newman, and he shares it all in *Do It! Speaking*. It's money-making idea after money-making idea in every single chapter."

—MARK HUNTER, CSP,
Author of *High-Profit Selling* and *High-Profit Prospecting*

"David Newman's *Do It! Speaking* is a miracle. Whether you're a beginner, seasoned CEO, or a Hall of Fame Speaker, this book is a must."

—MARK LEVY,
Founder of Levy Innovation LLC and Creator of Your Big Sexy Idea®

"If you are serious about professional speaking, then David Newman is the pro's pro!"

—JEFFREY HAYZLETT,
Primetime TV and Podcast Host, Hall of Fame Speaker,
Author, and Chairman of the C-Suite Network

"In this practical and rousing book, David Newman shows you how to take your speaking to the next level, along with your influence and success."

—TIM SANDERS,
New York Times Bestselling Author of *Love Is the Killer App* and *Dealstorming*

"The speaking business is tough. But if you're looking to gain more mind-share and market share for yourself, your company, or your brand, David Newman is an incredibly effective guide to help you chart your course."

—LIBBY GILL,
Author of *The Hope-Driven Leader* and
Capture the Mindshare and the Market Share Will Follow

"David Newman has written the most comprehensive book I have ever read on how to build, grow, and sustain a profitable speaking career."

—BARRY BANTHER, CMC, CSP,
and 2020–2021 President, National Speakers Association

"*Do It! Speaking* is your no-BS, real-deal guide to help you build your platform, expand your impact, and add a high-fee speaking profit center to your business right now."

—**JOEL BLOCK, CSP, MBA,** Founder of Bullseye Capital,
and Author of *Stop Hustling Gigs and Start Building a Business*

"David Newman is a marketing ninja! *Do It! Speaking* contains sage wisdom, brilliant insights, and countless tips that will show you how to bring in more business. Get it."

—**RANDY GAGE,**
Hall of Fame Speaker and Author of the *New York Times*
bestsellers *Risky Is the New Safe* and *Mad Genius*

"I've been in the speaking business for almost thirty years—and when David speaks, I listen. He'll help you expand your influence and fatten your wallet on every page of this great book. So what are you waiting for? Buy it already!"

—**KARYN BUXMAN,**
Neurohumorist, Hall of Fame Speaker, and Author of *Funny Means Money*

"David gives you the exact methodology, training, and tools to win more business, whether you've just started speaking or you're a seasoned pro."

—**STEPHEN SHAPIRO, CSP,**
Hall of Fame Speaker, and Author of *Best Practices Are Stupid*

"*Do It! Speaking* is filled with what David's paying clients value most—immediately actionable guidance to help you thrive as a speaking-driven expert."

—**LEANN THIEMAN, CSP,**
Hall of Fame Speaker, and *New York Times*
Bestselling Author of *Chicken Soup for the Nurse's Soul*

"Required reading for every speaker and every leader. *Do It! Speaking* is part marketing, part sales, and part high-energy wake-up call to help you achieve your leadership and sales potential."

—**BRIAN SMITH,**
Founder of UGG Australia and Author of *The Birth of a Brand*

DO IT!
SPEAKING

77 Instant-Action Ideas to Market, Monetize, and Maximize Your Expertise

DAVID NEWMAN, CSP

HarperCollins
Leadership

An Imprint of HarperCollins

Published by HarperCollins Leadership, an imprint of HarperCollins Focus LLC.

Any internet addresses, phone numbers, or company or product information printed in this book are offered as a resource and are not intended in any way to be or to imply an endorsement by HarperCollins Leadership, nor does HarperCollins Leadership vouch for the existence, content, or services of these sites, phone numbers, companies, or products beyond the life of this book.

Book design by Neuwirth & Associates.

ISBN 978-14002-1485-3 (eBook)
ISBN 978-14002-1484-6 (HC)

Library of Congress Control Number: 2019945835

Printed in the United States of America

19 20 21 22 23 LSC 5 4 3 2 1

CONTENTS

CONTENTS

PROLOGUE
PUBLIC SPEAKING:
THE ORIGINAL SOCIAL MEDIA

You're blogging. You're tweeting. You're linked in.
You're creating videos and articles and lead magnets.

All of that is great, but let's not forget that social media is—first and foremost—social! It's personal. And that person is YOU.

The ultimate test of a thought leader is the answer to one simple question: When you open your mouth, do people listen? Online, offline, in person, via email, via Skype, on SlideShare, on YouTube: The media doesn't matter. The messenger (YOU!) matters a whole lot more.

If Benjamin Franklin had social media, would he use it? You bet. Would it work for him? Absolutely. How can we be sure? Because when old Ben opened his mouth back in the 1770s and 1780s, people listened. The same could be said for Plato, Socrates, Shakespeare, Einstein, King, Jobs, and Obama.

 @dnewman

Long before social media, smart people rose to prominence using the influence of the spoken word.

Articulation of powerful ideas, useful ideas, crazy ideas, revolutionary ideas is what made people remarkable. Whether you stood up to speak to an audience of Roman senators, a rowdy bunch of war protesters, a roomful of hostile reporters, or a boardroom filled with naysayers, the people who made a difference did so because of the power of public speaking to spread their ideas and change the course of events.

Public speaking—the original social media—is based on the same principles as today's social media and online content marketing. The key factors to your success are:

1. Have something worth saying.
2. Say it in a powerful, simple, and intriguing way.
3. Deliver your message with consistency, clarity, and passion.
4. Change the game—don't blend in: stand out when you speak up.

Let's explore each of these in a bit more depth:

1. Have something worth saying. Craft your message by speaking to both the heart and the head. People are emotional creatures. Tap into emotion to back up your facts, opinions, and recommendations. As business author Harvey Mackay likes to point out, "There are no business relationships—all relationships are personal relationships."

2. Say it in a powerful, simple, and intriguing way. Don't mince words. Short sentences rule. People's attention spans are shrinking daily. Keep it short, snappy, and memorable. For example, when I speak on marketing, I use the power of alliteration by sharing my philosophy that marketing needs to be easy, effortless, and enjoyable. I call it the "three Es" and people remember it. Include hooks, taglines, and memory devices when you speak, and you will increase your influence and impact.

3. Deliver your message with consistency, clarity, and passion. Americans hate wafflers. Every political season, the worst you can call your opponent in a hotly contested election is a "waffler." It's considered even worse than lying! Don't be wishy-washy. Have a clear, strong point of view and hammer it home over and over: boldly, passionately, and fearlessly.

4. Change the game—don't blend in: stand out when you speak up. Boring doesn't sell. Boring ideas die. Boring people lose. In short, you want to be the opposite of boring. You want to stand out from the crowd.

Where can you zig where everyone else zags?

Where can you break the mold—or create a new mold that you (and you alone) are perfectly designed to fit in?

Those questions are exactly what this book is designed to help you answer.

This book is not for "dummies" because you're not a dummy. It's a book for smart people, but people looking for guidance, tips, and strategies, for insights, frameworks, and lasting principles for success—for people like YOU.

Ready? Here we go . . .

INTRODUCTION

Calling all speakers, executives, and entrepreneurs
who want to maximize their influence, impact, and income: YOU are in the
right place . . . or more accurately, you are reading the right book.

It all started with this passionate rant . . .

**If I see one more idiot posting about
"millionaire speaker" boot camps
or speak-to-sell megacourses, or
moronic pitches to "speak less and
earn more" as a paid professional
speaker, I'm going to pop an artery
because these are complete BS!!**

 @dnewman

You want the REAL secret to professional speaking success?
Great—here it is in three words: DELIVER. MASSIVE. VALUE.

Maybe four more words would help: WORK. YOUR. BUTT. OFF.

Listen, you're a smart cookie . . .

You know that true speaking success is about

* Impacting more people
* Increasing your income
* Building your credibility and authority

- ✹ Boosting your influence
- ✹ Signing up clients faster and more easily

As a full-time professional speaker who spent almost a full year "on the other side of the table" booking speakers for 160+ events, I can tell you this book will give you the keys to

- ✹ **Powerfully BRAND** your speaking business (from your "verbal business card" to your program titles, taglines, brands, and sub-brands so you get a focused, consistent, and irresistible package)
- ✹ **Precisely TARGET** your most relevant associations, groups, and conferences (so you stop spinning your wheels and build a strong foundation of credibility, repeatability, and referrability that becomes the basis for your "speaker booking machine")
- ✹ **Effortlessly CONNECT** you to your highest-probability prospects (who are eager to hear from you, look forward to your communications, and who consider you a true partner and not a peddler when it comes to solving their urgent, pervasive, and expensive problems)

Imagine you have X–ray vision into the speaking marketplace . . .

- ✹ You know the exact wants, needs, and urgencies of your most likely prospects.
- ✹ You STOP worrying about "convincing" association and corporate decisionmakers about the relevance and value in hiring you to speak.
- ✹ You wake up each morning knowing EXACTLY how and where to spend your energy in terms of marketing, writing, publishing, social media, relationship-building, networking, and any other method of business outreach.
- ✹ You instantly connect with meeting planners, conference producers, and corporate executives whose first reaction after thirty seconds on the phone with you is, "Yes—we want some of THAT!"
- ✹ You sit down each day at your computer armed with a clear game plan, a set of customized templates and proven scripts (in

your own voice), and a handpicked target list of prospects eager to hear from you so that marketing your speaking business becomes easy, effortless, and enjoyable (yes, REALLY!).

While that's a nice pipe dream, this book is the next best thing. This book is designed to help you generate real results—no theory, no fluff, and no bull. And more importantly, NO MORE "stupid sales tricks"—no more chasing disappearing prospects, and no more guessing and hoping and waiting for the phone to ring . . .

. . . instead you'll build a steady stream of well-qualified prospects and thrilled clients eager to hire you, rehire you, and enthusiastically refer your services to others.

 **@dnewman**

If you truly want to leverage your time, talent, content, expertise, and experience, you must master not only speaking, but marketing and selling too.

Even if you're NOT a full-time paid professional speaker, speaking to targeted groups of profit-rich audiences strengthens your marketing magnetism as an expert, consultant, or sales professional.

There is no magic bullet. There is no "millionaire speaker fairy." Get to work and you'll get results.

Ready to go behind the scenes? In these pages, you'll see not only how I built my own professional speaking practice, but, much more importantly, how I have helped hundreds of other speakers, executives, and experts just like you to do the same in our **Speaker Profit Formula** mentorship program. In fact, in the following pages, you're GETTING that same formula.

Nothing is assumed, and nothing is left out. You're getting exactly where to start and exactly what to do.

Step by step.

Day by day.

This book is for YOU—whether you're a seasoned professional speaker OR you are just starting to think about ways to speak more and get paid for it . . . you'll get dozens of instant-action ideas to begin using speaking as your #1 marketing tool for your business, your brand, and all your company's products, services, and programs.

If you're new to the speaking industry, you'll shave years off of your learning curve . . . and, if you're a seasoned speaker, this book may be the exact boost you've been looking for to launch (or relaunch) your business to its next level of success.

The real difference: We cross the chasm from *information to implementation* with real-world assignments that move you and your speaking business forward in tangible, specific ways. You'll be amazed at your own progress the moment you start following the steps outlined in these chapters.

COMMITTED TO YOUR SUCCESS

I am committed to making it possible for speakers, executives, and entrepreneurs like YOU to get the marketing tools, training, and support you need to make your speaking business more scalable, more profitable, and more successful.

That is why I wrote this book.

Everything is laid out for you—what to do and how to do it, what to say and how to say it to revitalize your speaking business OR to help you get it right the first time and give your speaking business the leverage, profits, clients, and recognition you deserve.

And this quick-take "small bites" format is designed to allow even super-busy professionals like you to get the marketing help you want—and to create a thriving business as an expert who speaks professionally.

Imagine once you start to consistently fill your calendar with perfect-fit speaking engagements . . .

* You'll know exactly the type of clients and audiences you want and where to find them.
* You'll get laser-focused on how to invest your time, effort, energy, and priorities.
* You'll be positioned as an expert.

- ✹ You'll feel extremely confident as your financial worries fade away.
- ✹ You'll crisply articulate how your programs help your clients.
- ✹ You'll do ONLY marketing tasks that you find easy, effortless, and enjoyable.
- ✹ You'll feel inspired, supported, and motivated to take action.

Put this book down right now and grab your FREE speaker marketing tools, templates, downloads, and companion tools at **www.doitmarketing .com/speak**.

You will see references to the specific tools, worksheets, and templates you need throughout the book, so you might as well log in, bookmark the resources page, and have everything at your fingertips. You'll also get the **"21-Day Speaker Marketing Playbook"** to create your perpetual marketing plan once you finish reading this book.

If you and your business are ready to kick some serious ass using the power of speaking, let's get this party started. **Strap in, hang on—and let's DO IT!**

 **1 STOP THE CRAZINESS!**

You've never been busier, and by busier I don't mean with well-paid speaking gigs jamming your calendar. I mean scrambling to market yourself: sending emails, writing blogs, updating your website daily, making phone calls. You're so busy, you're overwhelmed and yet you're just getting nowhere fast. Why?

Because you're reaching for the *tactical* tool kit without having a well-thought-out or even a completely-thought-out speaker marketing *strategy*.

Underline the word *strategy*, two or three or four times, or circle it with a big red Sharpie.

 @dnewman

Tactics without strategy creates busywork and overwhelm *and craziness*.

It's time to stop the craziness. It's time to develop a targeted, specific strategy carefully designed around what you want to say and what you want to sell.

The first step in developing your strategy is to decide on your **business model** and **revenue model** and **speaking model**: How will you structure your speaking-driven business and how will you make money from it? In the spirit of "walk before you run, and run before you fly," below are the four questions that will build the foundation for your speaker marketing strategy.

Even before we answer those four questions, let me give you a piece of advice:

It's Not Going to Happen by Accident!

No matter what outcomes you want to create from your speaking, **it's not going to come together without a plan**.

No one wakes up one day, totally out of the blue, and thinks, "Wow, I'm sitting on a half-million-dollar business, I've got three trainers on staff and I've got all these keynotes booked, I wrote these bestselling books and all these products I'm selling online, and I have no idea how it happened—gosh, isn't this a nice surprise?

2 YOUR STRATEGY IN FOUR QUESTIONS

Now that we have that straight, let's talk about the four fundamental questions you need to ask yourself before you can start designing and developing your speaker marketing strategy.

QUESTION 1:
WHAT ARE YOU BUILDING?

The first question is: **What's the empire that you're building?** The great thing about a speaking-driven business is that there are about a thousand different business models you can create. The problem? Only about five hundred will work for you, the other five hundred won't, and it's up to you to DECIDE what you really want to make happen!

* Are you building an organization?
* Are you building a lifestyle business?
* Are you building a solo practice?
* Are you building a consultancy?
* Are you building a thought-leadership empire that is someday going to be sold?

* Is there an exit strategy?
* Are you looking at building a brand that's larger than yourself with possibly licensing or certifying other people?
* Are you building something completely different? Is it a hybrid? Is it some mash-up of several of these models?
* Are you looking to leave your corporate job and launch your speaking full-time—or stay and enhance your "career insurance" by becoming the face and voice of your company's products, services, and brand?

QUESTION 2:
WHAT KIND OF WORK DO YOU WANT TO DO?

The second question to ask in designing and developing your speaker marketing strategy is: **What type of work do you want to do?**

You want to be a speaker but there are people who are **just all about the keynote**, there are people who are **just all about the half-day and full-day seminar**, there are others who only want to do two- or three- or five-day retreats, others who primarily want to consult, coach, facilitate, or do virtual programs.

Think about what kind of work you want to do: What's the length? What's the format? Think in terms of YOUR preferred depth, duration, and detail.

What format(s) do you want to "own"? Another way to approach this question is to ask yourself, "In which formats am I truly a rock star?" Focus on those—and let the other formats and delivery modes go. They're not for you. Your house—your rules!

QUESTION 3:
HOW MANY DIFFERENT REVENUE STREAMS DO YOU WANT?

The third strategy-building question to ask is: **What are the different revenue streams that you want?**

What are the different *active* revenue streams you want to pursue, meaning that you're exchanging your physical time, attention, and presence to generate that money?

What are the different *passive* revenue streams? Although, let me let you in on a little secret:

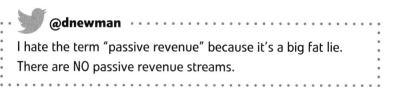

@dnewman

I hate the term "passive revenue" because it's a big fat lie. There are NO passive revenue streams.

I cringe when people use terms like "passive revenue," "make money in your jammies," or "earn money while you sleep." It implies you just stand there and collect the money. In fact, there's no such thing as passive revenue; that's a myth. There is revenue that you have to really work hard for in an *active* way, but you can monetize your content in a way that is **separate** from your personal time, attention, and presence.

In other words, you build it once and you sell it multiple times. **That may be leverage but it's not passive.**

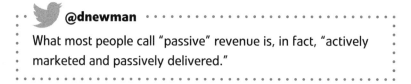

@dnewman

What most people call "passive" revenue is, in fact, "actively marketed and passively delivered."

QUESTION 4:
WHAT ARE YOUR DIFFERENT DELIVERY MODES?

The fourth question to ask in building your speaking-driven platform is: **What delivery modes will you use?**. In the mix of passive and active revenue sources that you've decided on, how much, if any, is going to be

* Speaking?
* Training?
* Coaching?

* Consulting?
* Facilitation?
* Products?
* Books?
* Online courses?

There are MANY options here. To get the complete list, download your free copy of the companion tool **"50 Shades of Pay"** from www.doit marketing.com/speak.

CREATE A ROUGH ROAD MAP

The purpose of these four questions is to help you sketch out some rough goals and a game plan. Don't get all caught up writing a seventeen-page strategic business plan. Simply jot some ideas down in a notebook or journal right now, or make yourself a short four-to-seven slide PowerPoint deck to keep handy; this will give you a road map and compass so that you know what you're building and you stay focused on where you're ultimately going.

3 WHAT IS YOUR TOPIC NICHE?

Now that you have a general idea of the structure of your speaking-driven business, the next step is to **find your best-fit clients and audiences**.

Creating a clear path to ideal clients requires pinpointing three things:

1. Your topic niche
2. Your target market
3. Your identity

We'll unpack each of these in order, starting with *topic niche*.

Topic niche is about your expertise. Topic niche is about **what is the slice of the universe, the slice of the encyclopedia of knowledge that you want to be**. About what are you the true go-to expert and standout authority?

Decide who you are: What's the "label" you want to put on your bottle? Negotiations speaker, customer service speaker, sales speaker?

Don't be afraid to specialize and focus your speaking-driven business on mastering ONE topic. ONE.

If you offer everything to everyone, you're like an **average** Chinese restaurant.

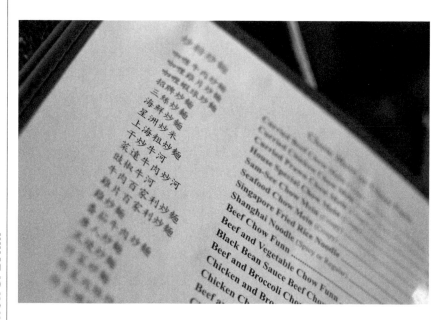

The menu has a million choices, and nothing is particularly good.

But now think of your **favorite** Chinese restaurant where you walk in and you always order the same thing because it's OUTSTANDING. Now, that Chinese restaurant stands out in your mind as THE place to go for your favorite dish. You've probably told ten friends how great this restaurant is—and you certainly told them what to order there and how delicious it is. My point—specialize and stick with it.

@dnewman

Don't be afraid of labels. Meeting planners BUY labels! Label yourself early on and focus on getting expertise that is DEEP rather than BROAD.

Wannabes know ten topics one-foot deep. Experts know one topic ten-feet deep—and beyond!

Think in terms of looking at your life in hindsight:
* what you're doing professionally right now
* all your past jobs, all your past careers, what you went to school for
* all the things that people say you're naturally great at
* all of your combined talents, wisdom, experience, expertise

And what's the low-hanging fruit? Where do you have the best names to drop and the best stories to tell?

If you have experience, if you have indisputable points of proof in a given industry, with a given target market, if you have testimonials, references, people that know you, love you, would gladly take your phone call, would welcome your name in their email inbox, how can you leverage those assets and relationships? That leads us right into your target market. Let's tackle that next . . .

4 WHAT IS YOUR TARGET MARKET?

Now you have to nail down your *target market*.

There are four keys to success for identifying your target market. **If you're missing any ONE of these four keys, you're in for a long, hard road.**

This might be why you've been struggling, why you're beating your head against the brick wall. That can end right now.

THE FOUR KEYS TO NAILING DOWN YOUR TARGET MARKET

1. Do You Have Access?

Do you have access to that target market?
   Can you get access to that target market?
   Can you buy a list?
   I'm not saying you should buy a list and spam the universe. You should not.

However, the definition of a **well-defined target market** is that you could go online to a list broker or database marketing firm and, for example, ask them to find *every technology company that has more than five million dollars of revenue.*

That is a clear, well-defined target market.

You could narrow your search even further and ask to find **the VP of sales in every five-million-dollar-plus technology company on the West Coast of the United States.**

If you can articulate it like that, you have an accessible target market.

Don't try to market to everyone. You can't boil the ocean.

 **@dnewman**

Speakers who target a well-defined slice of the universe have a vastly increased chance of success.

2. Is Your Topic Relevant?

The second key to help you zero in on your target market is relevance.

And by the way, relevance is not in *your* eyes, it's in *their* eyes.

If you're not seen as relevant, it doesn't matter how targeted or valuable you think your offerings might be. There's no sale.

It's also important to note that commodity information rarely has relevance. If they can find the same information you're sharing in your speeches on Google, in blog posts, and in YouTube videos, then you're not a thought leader—you're a thought follower and that's bad.

What's the alternative? Take a stand on your topic: Be unique.

Gary Markle is an HR and performance management consultant whose program is based on the idea of "No More Performance Reviews"; Alfie Kohn is a rewards and recognition expert who firmly believes that "Rewards don't work"; Larry Winget calls himself the Pitbull of Personal Development® and one of his books is titled *Shut Up, Stop Whining, and Get a Life*.

Remember: Sacred cows make the best steak.

 **@dnewman**

If you don't risk turning some people off, you'll never turn anybody on.

Be contrarian and event producers will remember you. Sound different and BE different. The more you stand out from the crowd in both style and substance, the more your audiences will remember you—and that's key for both RETENTION and REFERRALS. If you *sound* like every other speaker and you *act* like every other speaker and you *look* like every other speaker, you're making it very hard for clients and audiences to remember you—and you're making it even harder for them to REFER you!

3. Is There a Desire for Your Topic?

Are you tapping into an existing desire? Is it specific to and for a certain audience?

In other words, are your prospects already *actively looking* for the kinds of solutions that you and your programs and your speeches and your seminars provide?

Here's a big shift that will instantly increase your prospect's desire for what you do: SPECIFICITY.

Specific topics beat general topics—"Sales Success Secrets" isn't nearly as good as *"Overcoming the Stall: How to Shift Your Prospect Out of Neutral."*

"How to Become a More Effective CFO" isn't nearly as relevant as *"Seven CFO Negotiating Strategies for Vendor Contracts."*

TIP: Use the word FOR in your speech titles to target a specific audience:

* Presentation Skills **for** HR Executives
* Upselling **for** Customer Service Reps
* Internet Marketing **for** Real Estate Pros
* Leadership Essentials **for** Nurse Managers
* Lead Generation **for** Consulting Firms

This does two things for you—it makes your title more specific AND it identifies your target audience. Another bonus: The more specific your topic, the less you can be compared with the sea of generalist jack-of-all-trades speakers who are perceived—accurately—as a commodity.

 @dnewman

Be the aspirin for the headache that they already know they have.

4. Can You Dollarize Their Problem?

Finally, you need to articulate the *financial value* that you can deliver (called "dollarizing") to show your prospects and clients the true cost of their problem and the true value of solving it faster, better, or smarter than they're doing now.

And by the way, you can dollarize any speaking topic, including

* Leadership
* Sales
* Customer service
* Teamwork
* Technology
* Employee engagement
* Innovation
* Health and wellness
* Conflict resolution
* Diversity and inclusion
* Time management
* Strategic planning
* Communication skills
* And ANY so-called "soft" or squishy topic (love, happiness, motivation, etc.)

People tell me all the time, "Hey, David, that's easy for you to say because you're in marketing. And for marketing and sales experts, that's a straight shot to the bottom line, but MY topic doesn't work that way."

Confession time: It might be **easier** for a marketing speaker or sales speaker . . . but I've helped clients in every imaginable topic, in every imaginable industry to dollarize their value and their solutions so that their speaking fees (often $10,000 to $15,000—some even higher) **become inconsequential** compared to the **payoff** that the client gets as a result of their program.

HINT: **You don't need to tell them how valuable your programs are, they need to tell you**—and they need to be able to put a number on it—so that your fee becomes a little tiny dwarf compared to the number and the value and return on investment that your program delivers.

To download a fresh minty copy of the **"Money Machine Worksheet"** to help you dollarize your keynotes, seminars, and trainings, visit www .doitmarketing.com/speak.

5 WHAT IS YOUR IDENTITY?

TAKE THE CNN TEST

When you're on CNN, they put that red bar at the bottom of the screen. They give your name, and you get three or four words maximum. For instance, if I were on CNN, it would say my name and "Speaker Marketing Expert." What will be your two or three words?

* Sales Expert
* Leadership Speaker
* IT Security Consultant
* Futurist Author
* Executive Coach

Here's the problem: It's NOT going to say: *Sales and Leadership and Customer Service and Innovation and Hiring and Firing and Basket-Weaving and Boat-Building Expert.*

There just isn't room.

What are the "two seconds" of labeling and positioning that you want to convey? Fill in the blank with some possibilities here and see which one(s) you like best:

_____ Expert

_____ Speaker

_____ Consultant

_____ Author

_____ Coach

BUYERS BUY BOXES

Buyers buy boxes. We have to label ourselves incredibly clearly in the marketplace so that clients can buy the box that we're in.

Once you clearly label your category of expertise, only then should you worry about the distinction—then you can fret over your branding, then you can share about how you are faster, smarter, better, and cooler than anyone else who does what you do. But initially you must put yourself *in a category* just like books go on a specific bookshelf in the bookstore or wines go into a specific section in the liquor store.

6 IF YOU WANT TO DRIVE THE BMW, YOU NEED TO MASTER THE GNW (+U)

Your speaking success is a combination of your target market, your topic niche, your focus, your buyer persona, and your audience. And you want your prospects to slap their foreheads and say:

"I get it, I totally GET it. In fact, not only do I get it, we were just talking about this at our board meeting, so we NEED it. Not only do we need it, it's such a smart, relevant, appealing package that we WANT it."

Get it, Need it, Want it = GNW.

And the magic happens when they get it, need it, and want it with **urgency**.

So it's GNW + U.

How do you get to GNW? The first step is to be crystal clear. If you want to be successful:

* You cannot afford to confuse your target market.
* You cannot afford to confuse your message.
* You cannot afford to confuse your topic niche.
* You cannot afford to confuse your value, impact, and outcomes.

 @dnewman
You need to be a laser beam that cuts through the fog.

If you put that laser beam right up next to a piece of sheet metal, it cuts through it like butter. You are not going to cut through by being vague, by being safe, or by hedging your bets. You've got to be laser-focused and crystal clear.

7 THE BIGGEST MARKETING MISTAKE SPEAKERS MAKE

Let's talk more about the GNW + U crowd—the "get, need it, want it" buyers who are not only willing, but in fact *expecting*, to pay you premium fees for your work.

Here's a deep philosophical sound bite. Ready?

@dnewman

There's a difference between a market and an audience.

As a speaker, consultant, thought-leading executive, or entrepreneur, you may have heard about the importance of building an audience for your work . . . sounds great.

But it's nowhere as important as developing a market for your expertise.

You can spend YEARS attracting and serving an audience that is NOT your market. And that's just sad, painful, and frustrating.

These are as pernicious as they are deceptive.

WHICH of these has been holding you back—confusing you—or set you to wondering how come you're not making more money?

Here are seventeen vital differences between a market and an audience. Let's go down the list . . .

1. An **audience** listens. A **market** pays attention.
2. An **audience** wants entertainment. A **market** wants to solve problems.
3. An **audience** values an experience. A **market** values expertise.
4. An **audience** wants to watch. A **market** wants to act.
5. An **audience** wants information. A **market** wants implementation.

6. An **audience** reacts. A **market** responds.
7. An **audience** wants their questions answered. A **market** wants their answers questioned.
8. An **audience** wants you to be popular. A **market** wants you to be right.
9. An **audience** asks, "What can you do?" A **market** asks, "What's next?" and "What else?"
10. An **audience** says, "Great show!" A **market** says, "Great job!"
11. An **audience** tells their friends. A **market** tells their boss.
12. An **audience** buys your book. A **market** reads your book.
13. An **audience** likes your ideas. A **market** implements your ideas.
14. An **audience** wants your autograph. A **market** wants to give you their signature.
15. An **audience** applauds. A **market** refers.
16. An **audience** says, "Thank you." A **market** says, "Thank goodness!"

And finally—most important of all—read this next one as often as you need to:

17. An **audience** will HEAR you. A **market** will PAY you (well, often, and gladly).

Expert marketers not only build an audience—they develop a market for their value, ideas, products, services, and programs.

You may have an audience, an audience that is not able or willing or interested in paying money. For example, I have a client in Buffalo, New York, and she says to me, "Oh, David, I just can't get out of Buffalo. All I'm getting are these low-fee and no-fee gigs, $200 down at the chamber, $300 in church basements." And I say to her, **"That's not the problem; the problem is that you're taking them!"**

She had an audience. But she didn't have a market.

A market is willing to pay money. If you say, "I have a target market," that means that you've got buyers with money.

If you have an audience, then you have people who are willing to sit on their hands and listen for either no money or little money, and they're playing on their smartphones or whatever while you're talking. **That's not a market.**

That's why a lot of speakers are scratching their heads, thinking, "What's the problem? These people love me." Bad news: *The wrong people love you.* People with no money love you. The broke people love you.

> 🐦 **@dnewman**
>
> You don't want broke people to love you. You want check-writing entities to love you.

I want corporations and associations and nonprofits and the government and whomever you want to serve who's got a checkbook—I want *them* to love you.

When you say, "But, David, I have an audience and they love me," I always ask, **"Have you taken that love to the bank?"**

Fortunately, after many years, I have now figured out and I have helped hundreds of my clients figure out how to get the love *and* the money.

It's not ALL about the money, **but without the money**, there's nothing. No impact. No influence. No helping the people you want to help. No serving the people you want to serve. Because if you don't make money in your speaking-driven business, you'll eventually throw in the towel, put on the green apron at Starbucks, and get busy making lattes and Americanos. I take mine black, thanks!

> 🐦 **@dnewman**
>
> If your clients and audiences love you with no money, that's not real love.

If they love you with the money, that's real love. I'm not a relationship therapist but I'm guessing this is similar to love without sex and sex without love. You want both.

(And I'm going to stop here, because I'm in trouble already. The HR and "politically correct" police are coming after me right now. Gotta run!)

8 IT ALWAYS, ALWAYS STARTS WITH *WHO*

How do you find that niche market, the people with the money and the love?

Most executives and entrepreneurs start by thinking about their marketing—their website, video, what should they say in that next email, what should they say in their newsletter, what should they blog about, what should they post, what should they livestream, *WHAT SHOULD THEY DO?*

But that is the completely wrong question, or at least it's the completely wrong *first* question.

As I mentioned in my earlier book, *Do It! Marketing*, successful marketing always starts with your *who*, it always starts with who's the person who's got the love, who's got the money, and who's problem you're brilliant at solving.

The first question to ask yourself is, "Who am I talking to?" Let me give you a quick example of why this is important . . .

9 WRITE YOUR LETTER TO AUNT SALLY

Imagine that I ask you to take out a blank piece of paper. The assignment is: You're going to write a letter.

In the upper left-hand corner of the letter, I want you to write the word "Dear."

The very first thing you would ask me in order to go any further in that letter writing assignment is, *David, who am I writing to? Am I writing to my boss? Am I writing to an old girlfriend? Am I writing to my aunt Sally?*

I'm going to answer that for you so you can move forward with your assignment: You're writing to your aunt Sally.

Now, the top of your letter says, "Dear Aunt Sally."

At this point you might look up again and ask, *David, why am I writing to my aunt Sally? Am I writing to check on her health? Am I writing to thank her for that wonderful argyle sweater that she got me for my birthday? Am I writing to ask for her delicious cherry pie recipe from last Thanksgiving?*

Just so you can complete the assignment, my response is: You are writing to ask her for the delicious cherry pie recipe from last Thanksgiving.

Now you have the *who* and you have the *why*.

If I just cut you loose with those two pieces of information, most people would have no problem writing that letter:

> *Dear Aunt Sally,*
>
> *Hey, it was so great to see you and Uncle Bob at Thanksgiving. That cherry pie you make is always so delicious.*
>
> *I'd really love to get the recipe. Could you please send that to me?*
>
> *Love, Susan—and Cousin Earl says hello.*

Maybe a tiny percentage of people might ask, *David, how should I phrase the letter? What should the first sentence be?* But 99 percent of folks would have no problem writing that letter.

Now I want you to think about your website, think about your emails, think about your speaker one-sheet, think about what you say on the phone, think about what you say on LinkedIn, think about what you say face-to-face in a networking situation.

Everybody wants to know, *What do I say? What words do I use? What's the best headline? What's the right subject line?*

But you have no idea **who** you're writing to and you have no idea **why**. And you wonder why marketing is so hard.

Marketing is hard because you're trying to write to Aunt Sally, but you have no idea who Aunt Sally is. And you don't even know what you're asking her for!

Once you nail down the who and once you nail down the why, everything becomes easier.

You literally unlock the floodgates; you are never lost for words. You know exactly what to say and how to say it. You know what to send, you know how to have the marketing conversation and the enrollment conversation, you know their heartaches and headaches and challenges and gaps.

You can **articulate clearly and explicitly and succinctly** how you can solve either their problems or their audience's problems.

And it always starts with who.

10 FIND YOUR "HUNGRY" MARKET

When Ray Kroc, the founder of McDonald's, was asked about the secret to his success, he thought for a moment and then replied, "Well, I think the biggest secret to my success is that nobody ever walked into one of my restaurants who wasn't hungry."

After some reflection, you may come to realize that you have to repackage and reposition your expertise for a hungry market.

I'll give you a couple of examples. You might say, "I'm a presentation skills expert, and *everybody* needs better presentation skills." And I'm going to agree with you. Everybody does need better presentation skills.

But can you market to *everybody*? No, you cannot, so stop trying.

 @dnewman

EVERYONE is not a good target market—nor are they equally hungry for what you have to offer. Market to the non-hungry and you starve.

Who Suffers More Greatly, Who Needs It More Desperately?

Those are the key questions you have to ask. Whether your topic is sales, leadership, humor, innovation, there is a specific group that needs your solution more urgently, that suffers from that problem more greatly, and that will value you more highly.

Let's stick with presentation skills as our example. Who is absolutely the worst at presentation skills? Not to pick on anybody, but I'm going to say it's actuaries, or maybe it's engineers, maybe it's accountants. It's all these people who are so deep into their left brain that making a presentation, building rapport, making eye contact, and relating to an audience of humans is nowhere near their comfort zone. And they're terrible at it when they try.

What if you decide to serve that exact market—the folks who suffer from the problem more greatly, who need it more desperately and who would value it more highly?

Stop being a presentation skills expert for the universe and you can start being the presentation skills expert for that hungry target market.

Think about how you can thin-slice the market. How can you find the real urgency?

Remember: Everyone is NOT a target market, nor is everyone equally *hungry*.

Everyone doesn't buy. *Somebody* **buys. Specific programs sell.**

"Everyone" does not have a checkbook, "everyone" doesn't have a credit card, but *somebody* does.

Somebody buys, which means that *specific* programs sell. Specific solutions to specific problems.

And if you identify your hungry market that suffers from it more greatly, needs it more desperately, and has bigger pains, problems, heartaches, and headaches than everybody else, *those are your highest-probability, highest-value prospects.*

Those are the same people who are willing to buy more. They spend more, they decide faster, get off the fence, rarely drag their feet, and are much more likely to refer you and pass you around like candy if they love your work.

 **11 BUILD YOUR MARKETING LANGUAGE BANK**

"Marketing Language Bank" is a term I first shared

in my previous book, *Do It! Marketing*. It includes **every piece of marketing language** you use online, offline, orally, and in writing, and that includes:

* every headline
* every sound bite

- every proprietary "you-ism"
- everything you're known for saying
- your marketing conversations
- your sales conversations
- what you blog about
- your email subject lines
- what you livestream about
- what's on your business card
- what's on your speaker one-sheet
- what's on your website
- what's on your social media profiles
- what you say when people ask you what you do

All of those things collectively are your marketing language bank.

If you don't nail that language, you're not going to attract the right kinds of people and you're going to be stumbling and fumbling and bumbling.

The payoff? **Once you've developed and fleshed out your marketing language bank, you will never be facing a blank screen again.**

Because it's all going to be prewritten and ready to go. How cool is that?

DO IT! SUCCESS STRATEGY: PROSPECTS NOT REPLYING? HERE'S HOW TO FOLLOW UP MORE EFFECTIVELY, AND CLOSE MORE QUICKLY

BY ART SOBCZAK

One of the biggest challenges that speakers, trainers, and consultants have is with prospects not responding to their calls and messages.

To compound that, they don't often realize they are causing that to happen.

Let's explore this.

(continues)

Do you really know where you stand with the prospects in your follow-up files right now?

Come on, really now?

I'm not trying to make you feel bad, but my experience is that many speakers have **no clue** where they are in the sales process with a majority of the people they are following up with.

Yet, they continue to call, continue to leave voice-mail messages (*"Hey, I'm just checking in with you, wondering how it's going . . ."*), continue to email (*"Did you see my last email?"*), and **hope** that something will happen.

It's like running on a treadmill.

Except it hurts more than helps.

Here's why:

1. **Repeated messages with no value position you as a vendor . . . a salesperson whose goal is to sell them something.** The more you call to "just check in," the more the image of the "stalker salesperson" is solidified in their mind.

2. **You waste time and money.** Many of these "prospects" you're chasing will never hire you. You're throwing away time—which translates into money—by continuing to call them. Not only are you wasting time when you DO reach them, but factor in all of the attempts and messages you leave.

And then add the prep time for each call. (You are doing pre-call planning, right?)

OK, so what should we be doing?

Let's zoom in to a call. We need to gauge the temperature of the prospect and get a snapshot of precisely where we are with them.

I've found that it's always best to let the prospect tell you their perception of the progress of the sales cycle and what the next steps should be.

For example, when you reach the point where you feel things have moved sufficiently, ask:

* "So, where are we right now?"
* "Where do we sit right now?"
* "How far do you feel we have progressed to this point?"
* "How close are we to making this happen?"
* "What are the next steps?"
* "What next?"
* "What needs to happen on your end to move forward?"
* "How do you see us proceeding?"

Assuming you've done this, received good information, and the person truly is a good prospect, then what?

The success of the follow-up is in direct relation to the success of the previous call, and what is to happen next.

Always get a commitment that they (the prospect) **will do something** and you'll **do something** as a result of the call.

Then you can follow up with:

"I'm calling to continue our conversation of last week where we had discussed _____ and you were going to review the sample videos and workbook materials I sent you. I'd like to go through those with you and I have some additional information about a couple of hot topics in your industry I believe you'll find beneficial."

Don't assume your prospect is in the same frame of mind as you when you call. Actually, you should assume they might not even remember you. Briefly review where you left the previous conversation: **"The last time we spoke, you had shown interest in . . ."**

"I'm calling to continue our conversation from last week where we had discussed _____ and you were going to . . ."

(continues)

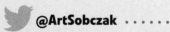

> **@ArtSobczak**
>
> When it comes to sales follow-ups, activity is not
> accomplishment.

Use these ideas to move your prospects forward, and you will fill your calendar.

Art Sobczak helps sellers get through, get in, and sell using conversational, commonsense sales and prospecting processes and messaging. He's the author of the award-winning book Smart Calling: Eliminate the Fear, Failure, and Rejection from Cold Calling. *Get free tips on prospecting and "selling without rejection" at SmartCalling.com. Listen to his value-packed podcast at TheArtOfSales.com.*

12 THE MAGICAL POWER OF DECIDING

DECIDE is the most powerful word in marketing.

Decide who you are.
Decide who your prospects are.
Decide to do your best work.
Decide not to work with jerks.
Decide on your menu of investable opportunities.
Decide what business model you're running.
Decide what revenue model your pricing comes from.

Decide what tasks can be delegated, eliminated, or outsourced.

Decide to pursue a niche market.

Decide to publish content regularly.

Decide to become a valued asset to your prospects.

Decide to become indispensable to your clients.

Decide to make a bigger splash in a smaller (or bigger) pond.

Decide what kinds of projects are NOT for you.

Decide on your marketing strategy.

Decide on a small, focused set of tactics.

Decide to market more consistently.

Decide to sell more bravely.

Decide to dream bigger.

Decide to act faster.

Decide to crush it.

AND.

YOU.

WILL.

 # 13 WHAT'S YOUR MISSION FOR TODAY?

Nope, this is NOT about that kind of soft, squishy "mission-vision" thing. . . . This is about what's on your plate right now, today, right this minute.

My friend Jose Palomino, a marketing expert with ValueProp.com, sent me an email about some website tweaking that he was doing that day. He wrote, "Getting the timing right and the sliders to stop rotating after the final reveal is today's mission."

Bam—that was his ONE thing for the day.

Was he doing other tasks? You bet. Was he developing business, calling clients, following up on sales leads, and doing paperwork? Sure . . . but he also had his "mission" for the day.

When it comes to your success as a speaking-driven professional, you have a million things to do and a hundred priorities.

Wouldn't having a SINGLE mission for the day be great?

Well . . . you can. Many important tasks can be done in as little as fifteen minutes and tackling ONE head-on might be exactly what you need to regain that most precious entrepreneurial asset: MOMENTUM.

Some examples to get you started:

* Revise your home page copy.
* Write an important email to a client or prospect.
* Send an invoice you've been procrastinating on.
* Post a blog.
* Submit an article to a trade journal or industry publication.
* Respond to a media request.
* Send out your email newsletter.
* Circle back with a prospect who's on the fence.
* Clean up your LinkedIn profile.
* Post a long-overdue recommendation on LinkedIn.
* Send a thank-you note.
* Mail a book to a prospect, influencer, or decisionmaker.
* Pick up the phone and apologize to someone important.
* Ask for that referral you've been shy about pursuing.
* Contact that virtual assistant you've been thinking of hiring.
* Post your internship job description with your local university.
* Begin a research file or a Google Doc for your next book.
* Make a list of twenty companies you'd like to speak for or consult with.
* Clear off your desk (you can do this in five minutes if you create a file folder called "Crap from Desk" and today's date!).
* Do a competitive sweep and see who's doing what in your industry so you can refresh your offerings.
* Shoot a two-minute video and post it to LinkedIn, Facebook, and YouTube.

- Erase the whiteboard in your office and create a "fresh start."
- Take yourself out to a coffee shop for a two-hour strategic meeting with yourself, a legal pad, and a pack of Sharpies.
- Take a nature walk and bring your pocket audio recorder or smartphone to capture ideas.
- Reconnect with an old client, friend, or colleague.
- Write an Amazon book review for a book you admire in your field.
- Call your tech wizard to fix a nagging technology problem you've been tolerating for way too long.
- Leave a forty-five-second voice mail for a client just to say how much you value your relationship with them.
- Visit your favorite bookstore and buy a magazine to flip through for new business ideas.

@dnewman

What's YOUR mission for today?

DO IT! SUCCESS STRATEGY: BUILD AN INTERNATIONAL FOLLOWING FAST

BY DEBBIE ALLEN, CSP

If you are already established as a professional speaker and have a solid business and brand foundation online, you are in a great position to build your international following very quickly.

Why not consider setting up your own international speaking tour?

As a professional speaker, I rarely do vacation travel on my own dollar. When I want to visit a country, I search online for speaking opportunities in that area of the world and get booked to speak most of the time.

(continues)

While I'm in that part of the world, I will add on additional travel and vacation days to experience the country and the culture.

This is exactly what I did when I decided that I wanted to experience New Zealand. I've always wanted to travel to New Zealand from the States. What I did next was rather gutsy to say the least, but it paid off for me.

I planned my own event with no database in that part of the world. First, I found a location to host my event in Auckland, New Zealand. I took a risk by signing the contract and making a commitment to host it—with no database!

Once the event and timeline where in place, I started marketing to get speaking engagements to set up my New Zealand tour. I easily booked six speaking engagements over a three-week period traveling in both North and South Island. Most of these were smaller groups of fewer than fifty people. Some were booked from meetup.com groups and others booked via Professional Speakers Chapters. Since I was offering to waive my speaking fee in exchange for promoting and selling my event from stage, it was easy to get the bookings.

These smaller events filled my database and my own event. It was a real win-win-win since the client got a world-class speaker at no cost to them (not even the cost of travel), I was able to fill my own event and create profits from it, and I got to travel and experience a new country at the same time.

It takes some courage to put on your own event and speaking tour (especially without a database there) but it can definitely pay off in a big way when developing international exposure fast.

***

Debbie Allen, CSP, is the bestselling author of The Highly Paid Expert and Insider Secrets of International Speaking *and* Success Is EASY. *Learn more about Debbie's professional speaking and business mentoring programs at DebbieAllen.com.*

14 PERFORMER, TEACHER, OR CATALYST?

Sometimes speakers are hired as a performer, sometimes they're hired as a teacher, and sometimes they're hired as a catalyst.

These are three different kinds of speakers.

They're typically hired by different kinds of buyers and the outcome and value proposition is also different.

A *performer's* **value proposition is about delivering an experience.** You're hired to create an experience of what happens in that meeting room during that forty-five- to ninety-minute speaking slot. Nothing before, nothing after, but oh man, during those ninety minutes, you take them on a ride, you take them on a journey. When they see your opening keynote, when they attend your main stage session, when they're all gathered together for that awards dinner, you blow their socks off. This category typically contains the juggler, the musician, the hypnotist, the purely "experiential" speakers.

The *teacher* is all about the content. You're hired for your expertise, insights, opinions, practices, principles, tools, tactics, and takeaways. This is also typically referred to as a "hard topic" speaker. If you wrote a great book on your topic, you're probably a teacher. If you convey a ton of how-to information, insights, and advice, you're probably a teacher. And if you cut your teeth in the world of corporate training (as I did), then you're definitely a teacher! One of my oldest friends introduced me to a new colleague this way: "Meet David Newman. He can't open his mouth without teaching." That was one of the best compliments I've ever received.

The *catalyst* is the spark for change, and thus it's more of a convening, facilitating, masterminding, or interviewing role. You might do live onstage interviews, you bring your own insights as you facilitate panels, or you do "onstage consulting," which is bringing your consulting skills to bear on specific situations in your talk, or as you answer audience questions, or as you facilitate "hot seats" with volunteers from the audience.

How would you articulate your mix? What percentage is the performer? What percentage are you a teacher? And what percentage do you feel you're a catalyst?

Performer: _____ %
Teacher: _____ %
Catalyst: _____ %

The reason you want to identify this NOW is so that the speaking gigs you go after and the speaking gigs **where it makes sense for them to hire you** are the ones where *what you deliver* is exactly what they want their audience's experience to be.

If you're a hysterically funny speaker, don't go after the content gigs or the catalyst gigs. If you're a pure content speaker, forget competing with the jugglers and the comedians. And if your real strength is as a catalyst, then don't worry about chasing the keynote gigs where it doesn't fit your strengths.

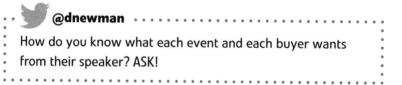

@dnewman

How do you know what each event and each buyer wants from their speaker? ASK!

For example: "I have a mix of motivation and content that I like to customize for each of my clients. On a scale of 0 to 100 percent, what percentage motivation would you like in this program and what percentage of content?"

Know your strengths—and then **let your buyer decide** how to deploy those strengths to serve their audience best.

DO IT! SUCCESS STRATEGY: LEVERAGING CLIENT ACQUISITION THROUGH VISTAGE SPEAKING

BY HENRY DEVRIES

Would you like to find a sponsor for your speaking?

As the CEO of Indie Books International, I work with consultants who want to attract high-paying clients by marketing with a book and a speech. To find clients, I sponsor small-scale seminars around the country for consultants that are no-cost to attend and no selling takes place. No cost. No selling. No kidding.

How can I afford to do this? I speak about twelve times a year for Vistage International. When Vistage sends me to a city to speak, say Atlanta or Sacramento, I stay an extra day to host my half-day "Marketing with a Book and Speech Summit." In essence, Vistage picks up the tab.

Vistage has one of the largest active speaker databases in the world, with more than a thousand experts speaking on topics from strategic planning to finance, sales, marketing, leadership, and work/life balance. You are paid a small honorarium ($500 to start) to speak for Vistage, plus modest travel expenses.

Some of the authors I have published have built their business around contacts made by speaking for Vistage. In addition to my client acquisition seminars, I have also picked up speaking gigs in the $5,000 to $10,000 range as a result of showcasing my speaking through Vistage. My topic is "Persuade with a Story!"

Founded in 1957, Vistage facilitates private advisory groups for CEOs, senior executives, and business owners. An exclusive community of more than 21,000 business leaders across a broad array of industries in sixteen countries, Vistage allows members to tap into different perspectives to solve challenges, evaluate opportunities, and develop strategies for better business performance. Most

(continues)

33

monthly meetings of eight to sixteen CEOs include a three-hour, interactive workshop presentation from an expert speaker.

There are three main reasons Vistage speaking might appeal to you:

1. You may desire to impact small-business CEOs, presidents, and owners and their companies.

2. You can sharpen your speaking skills in front of a highly demanding audience.

3. You gain business development and lead generation opportunities in the small-business space.

I interviewed Vistage CEO Sam Reese at a Vistage Speaker Appreciation Event in Denver. He was enthusiastic about the important role that Vistage speakers play in helping members transform their lives and grow their businesses.

"Our vision at Vistage is to be the world's most trusted advisors to CEOs and key executives to help them become more effective leaders, and this vision is only realized if our members achieve stellar results," Reese told me. "An analysis of Dun and Bradstreet data revealed that Vistage members grow their companies at three times the rate of an average US company. Vistage speakers help members to optimize their instincts, judgment, and decisionmaking, leading to lasting results."

Henry DeVries, cofounder and CEO of Indie Books International, speaks to thousands of businesspeople each year on how to persuade with a story. In his writing and speaking, he shares, in humorous ways, pragmatic strategies that can double sales results and achieve marketing returns of 400 percent to 2,000 percent. In the last ten years, he has helped ghostwrite, edit, and co-author more than three hundred business books, including his McGraw-Hill bestseller, How to Close a Deal Like Warren Buffett—*now in five languages, including Chinese. As a result of his work, consultants get the four Bs: more bookings, more blogs, more buzz, and a path and plan to more business. On a personal note, he is a baseball nut who has visited forty-two major league ballparks and has two to go before he "touches 'em all." His email is henry@indiebooksintl.com.*

15 YOUR COMPETITIVE SCAN

If you don't know who your competition is, how can
you position yourself to be distinct or MEANINGFULLY different from them?

 @dnewman

Know your competition because it's impossible to differentiate yourself against a question mark.

It literally is impossible to *differentiate* and *distinguish* and *dominate* unless you know who you're competing with.

Differentiation begins with knowing your competitors and becoming a student of the game.

Here's how:

STEP 1:
FIND FIVE TO SEVEN DIRECT AND
INDIRECT COMPETING OR ALTERNATIVE SPEAKERS.

These people can be **at your level**, they can be **slightly above your level** (meaning higher fee level, more fame, more notoriety, they've written more books, they're "more famous" in your niche), or they can be **emerging speakers**—they can be new up-and-comers but they at least *look like* they have their act together.

STEP 2:
WHAT ARE THEIR MESSAGES, METHODS, AND MODES?

Now make a grid to capture the key information on your competitors.

What are their messages, what are their key sound bites, what's in their marketing language bank, what are their delivery modes for their expertise, what are their target markets?

 @dnewman
Only by doing competitive speaker research can you separate yourself from the crowd.

If you say, "I never look at other leadership speakers. I'm a leadership speaker but I don't care what other leadership speakers are doing"—that's a real danger.

The danger is called blindness.

You're blind because without scanning the competitive landscape, you risk doing and saying the same things EVERY OTHER leadership speaker, consultant, and expert is doing and saying.

You might not know it, but you're using the same language, you're using the same terms, you preach the same mantras, maybe you've even read those other experts' books years ago and that language just seeped into your thinking . . . and now you're nothing but a cheap clone.

If you're not studying the competition, you risk becoming them, which is, of course, the *exact opposite* of differentiation and distinction and domination.

Here's a handy tool for you to capture notes as you do your competitive scan.

For a downloadable print-friendly copy of this worksheet, visit doit marketing.com/speak.

Competitive Scan Worksheet

	Comp1	Comp2	Comp3	Comp4
Speaker Name				
Website				
Brand(s)				
Methods/modes				
Target market				
Sound bites				
Value proposition				
Fee range				
Google results				
Articles				
Demo video				
Blog posts				
Sample clients				
LinkedIn URL				
Facebook				
Twitter				
YouTube				
Other key info				
Score (1–10)				

STEP 3:
HOW CAN YOU ZIG WHERE THEY ZAG?

Now that you know who the competition is and what they're offering, you can ask yourself: How can I go where they are not going? How can I be where they are not? How can I be meaningfully different, unique? **How can I zig where they zag?**

The goal: When prospects and clients see how you've positioned yourself, you want them to say: "Hang on, this speaker is different; this speaker is smarter, better, faster, cooler, more relevant, more valuable—**we have to hire this speaker right now**."

16 GOOGLE IS YOUR FRIEND!

Here's the good news: **Google is your friend.**
Here's how to use it:

> [Your topic] speaker
> [Your topic] expert
> [Your topic] consultant

For example—humor speaker, sales expert, social media speaker, leadership expert, team building consultant, entrepreneurship speaker, customer service consultant, small business marketing speaker, etc. There you have it: That's your competition.

How many results did you get?

You'll be amazed, you'll be astounded, and you're soon going to realize, "Oh my gosh, there are a million of me—there are a million social media speakers, there are a million marketing speakers, there are a million leadership speakers."

And I won't lie—at first, you're going to get depressed.

I want you to get a little depressed when you look at the competition because I want you to take the notion of "Cooler, Better, Faster, Smarter" seriously. The harsh truth is there's no room at the top for another "Same-o, Lame-o" speaker. You must stand out; that's the whole reason behind you becoming a student of the game and deeply understanding the field you're playing in.

But you have to know the competition. And here are some specific things to look for:

* Look at their articulation.
* Look at their value proposition.
* Look at their messaging.
* Look at their program titles.
* Look at their sound bites.
* Look at their keywords.
* Look at their catchphrases.
* Go to their website and watch their videos.
* Search them out on speaker's bureau websites.

Check them out thoroughly:

* Download their speaker one-sheet.
* Download their program descriptions.
* Look at their messaging, branding, titles, and positioning.
* Find them on LinkedIn—see what they're posting on LinkedIn, see what groups they belong to, read their written recommendations.
* Check out their Facebook profile, check out their Facebook business page. Their book might have a Facebook page or they may host a free group on Facebook. Watch any livestreams they've done over the past month or two.
* Find their Twitter account. What hashtags do they use? Who are they retweeting? What's the topic and tenor of their tweets? What content are they sharing?

* Find them on YouTube, watch their videos. Don't just watch their speaker demo video, watch their "talking head" videos, watch their content videos.
* Find them on SlideShare, find their presentations or white papers or ebooks.
* Find them on Amazon, find their self-published books, find their traditionally published books. Look at their Amazon author profile.

Now, this sounds like a lot of work. But remember: You're not doing this with fifty people or a hundred people. You're doing a deep-dive competitive scan with the four or five top names that continually come up. This is both a research exercise and an exercise in pattern recognition.

If you're already savvy with this, you probably know the two or three or four top names already. Even so, new folks are entering your field on a daily basis so you should also scan for newer folks—the up-and-comers, not just the old chestnuts who've been teaching and preaching in your field forever.

✓ 17 DEEPEN YOUR SEARCH

It's time to get creative with your online searching.

Put on your detective hat and answer questions such as: **Who are their clients, what do they write about, where do they publish articles?** Also find out **who is in their tribe**—what industries, what market segments, what niches, what vertical markets are they in?

Research, specifically, the associations, conferences, and companies they've served.

Find blogs, publications, trade journals, and association newsletters where their articles have appeared.

Now you can window-shop their clients. Some of those clients might make fantastic prospects for you.

Let's say you find that speaker on LinkedIn and they have twenty or thirty recommendations. If you're connected to them, you can see all of these including the specific executives at the specific companies who recommended them.

Now you can start "accidentally on purpose" connecting with people.

Accidentally on purpose join the same LinkedIn group, accidentally on purpose connect with these same clients on Facebook, accidentally on purpose start to go to the same industry and association meetings, accidentally on purpose start submitting your articles to those same exact publications.

You're going to organically appear on your new prospects' radar; you're going to show up in their world like a happy, squeaky wheel so in those niches, in those industries, for those buyers, pretty quickly, **the perception buyers will get about you is: "This person is everywhere. This person is ubiquitous, this person is preeminent."**

 @dnewman

You have to go narrow if you want to go deep. Big fish, small pond is good. ONLY fish, small pond is even better.

 **18 FIVE KEYS TO DEVELOPING YOUR UNIQUE MESSAGE**

1. **Go with what you know**—Look to your own education, background, experience, passions, or specialized skills.

2.   Tie it into an urgent, pervasive, and expensive problem or trend—For example, helping your business clients improve sales is always strong; helping them improve performance and productivity is always strong. Avoid fads or nontransferable expertise.

3.   Figure out what your prospects are ALREADY buying and position your speaking and other services into that same category— What are they currently investing money in that they think/hope will solve the same need as your programs or services?

For example, a social media speaker might specialize in an industry that's accustomed (or addicted) to Yellow Pages advertising because "you've always bought an ad." Don't make your prospects wrong—show them how a robust social media presence is "just like a Yellow Pages ad except it lives on the web and it's even better at capturing leads and converting them to sales."

Then take a look at conference websites, download conference brochures that list speakers and topics they've hired in the past, look at THOSE speakers' websites and topic lists. This might even add two or three names to the competitive scan that you just did!

4.   Market test your new messages/principles/angles informally with your business friends, employees, partners, and trusted advisors. Does your new speaking topic make sense to them? Do they find it appealing and effective in gaining attention? Is it relevant and complete? Does it reflect the current reality of their biggest pains, problems, challenges, and gaps?

For example, when I started mentoring speakers, consultants, and experts, I did not want to bill by the hour. One of my principles was:

"Unlike many other consultants, I'm more interested in getting you to your destination than in running the meter!"

Another sound bite from those early days was:

"Fixed fees. No surprises. Just results."

When I tested both those phrases with the folks I trust, their faces lit up and they immediately "got it." You could see it in their body language. That's the kind of reaction YOU want to get when you test yours!

5. **Call or meet with some actual buyers** and get their reaction (your industry contacts, clients, former clients, prospects). And no, this is not a sales gimmick. You really ARE simply "running some new ideas by them."

If you're not comfortable taking this approach because it sounds too much like asking for a favor (gasp!) then try this reversal technique: Tell them you have some new ideas and you'd like to get their help in "shooting some holes in them to see what I've missed." People love tearing down ideas (sad but true).

The only thing you're not telling them is that in the process of shooting all those holes in your speaker strategy, they are actually helping you to make it bulletproof!

DO IT! SUCCESS STRATEGY: THE POWER OF THE PEEC STATEMENT™

MICHAEL GOLDBERG, CSP

Every speaker, expert, and entrepreneur who actively networks and promotes their business is familiar with the "elevator speech." This is the thirty-second introduction used to explain what you do so others can help you. A good elevator speech should be light (not too much jargon or industry stuff), kind of fun (perhaps depending on your market), and memorable.

The *PEEC Statement™* or **P**rofession, **E**xpertise, **E**nvironments, and **C**all to Action is a great way to share what you do, whom you work with, and what you're seeking.

Here's how it works:

PROFESSION

This is a broad way of describing your role; it's not necessarily your title but it could be. For example, if you're a speaker or trainer, focus on who you help and what you help them with—just keep it simple:

(continues)

"I'm a consultant and the founder of Knock Out Networking! My focus is helping sales producers grow their business."

EXPERTISE

This speaks to the areas within your business where you have the most knowledge. Don't rattle off more than three areas of expertise because it may come across as trying to be all things to all people. Just talk about your top three favorites or where you think you have the most smarts. Of course, these may not be your only areas of expertise, but you wouldn't share everything on the first date, would you? Again, simple!

"My expertise is in the areas of networking, referrals, and recruiting."

ENVIRONMENTS

This is your target market or whom you serve best and therefore wish to serve most. What industry, profession, market segment, niche, demographic, dynamic, or geography reflects where you do your best and most fulfilling work? A typical concern of speakers and consultants (and most salespeople, too) is that you're limiting other opportunities but, in my experience, the exact opposite is true. People in other fields are attracted to you because you're a specialist and therefore you must be very good.

"Most of my work is (or "I'm establishing a niche") in the insurance and financial services industry with firms like ABC Financial Group and XYZ Insurance Company."

CALL TO ACTION

This is where you mention the types of introductions or information you're seeking. Keep in mind that you shouldn't make a strong request of those you're meeting at a networking event because they're not at the event to be sold your services. Also, you probably haven't established enough trust with them. Be specific about what you're looking to accomplish and who you're looking to meet. The more specific you are (names, titles, companies), the more successful you will be.

"I'm looking to meet managing directors and heads of distribution for investment firms like Morgan Stanley and Merrill Lynch. Any advice, insight, or recommendations you may have on how to make connections like this?"

Keep in mind that the *PEEC Statement* is a structure not a script. PEEC is simply a framework to keep your conversation focused. It should be prepared, not memorized. Just embrace the four concepts as bullet points and develop your language around it so it's conversational.

Deliver a prepared, powerful, and interesting *PEEC Statement* and enjoy the rewards of effectively promoting yourself, your brand, and your business.

Michael Goldberg, CSP, has helped thousands of sales producers generate hundreds of thousands of dollars to their bottom line. His firm, Knock Out Networking, is recognized as the speaking and training resource on networking to the insurance and financial services industry. Michael is a two-time TEDx speaker, writes numerous columns, is the author of the go-to book on networking for the industry, and has online programs that are licensed through corporate offices. Michael is an award-winning adjunct professor at Rutgers University and frequently volunteers as a speaker at organizations focused on career search. If you want Michael "in your corner," connect with him at KnockOutNetworking.com.

19 SEVEN REASONS TO OWN A NICHE

1. It's easier to be the expert.

It's easier for you to develop deep expertise in your favorite area and let everything else go.

2. It's easier to find buyers—and for them to find YOU!

It's easier to identify buyers, to target them, to reach out to them, to track them. It's easier to "accidentally on purpose" run into them on LinkedIn, at live conferences, at trade shows, and at industry events.

It's also easier to target your publishing strategy so that you're in the magazines that land on their desk every month.

For example, if you target the banking industry, you should be in the American Bankers Association magazine. Why? Because all bank presidents get one. It lands on their desks, *and most bank presidents read it.* They see your smiling face in there every month with a column on sales or leadership or team building or social media. Then when you call or you email, and you send them a copy of your book, they're 80 percent sold. Why? Because you're a columnist in the "authority publication" of their industry.

3. It's easier to position yourself above the generalists.

Once you dedicate yourself to dominating a slice of the marketplace, it's easier to position yourself above the generalists.

 @dnewman

"This is all I do" is one of the most powerful phrases you can ever say to a prospect.

You know what, Susan, I'm glad you called because this is all I do. I do this work morning, noon, and night; I eat [your topic] for breakfast, lunch, dinner, and a midnight snack. There is no area of this topic in which I can't dramatically improve the results for your audience.

You're not saying this in an arrogant, bloviated way. You're saying it as a factual statement because **if it's true** then there really is nobody better to hire than you.

4. Experts win on value; generalists die on price.

 @dnewman

If there are a million people who do what you do, buyers automatically start playing the "How low can we go?" game with your fees.

It becomes very hard to distinguish yourself with any type of effective marketing because by definition—all generalists look the same!

No specialization, no secret sauce, no compelling reason to do business with you.

On the other hand, if you're a fifth-degree black belt in your topic—you're truly THE go-to specialist in your area of expertise—then there will be a line of premium clients eagerly waiting to invest in your premium programs at a premium fee.

5. Alliances and referrals come easier.

More people will want to *refer, recommend,* and *partner* with you because they are not threatened with your overlap into their expertise.

If I sprang on the scene and said, "Hi, I'm David Newman. I do sales and marketing and leadership and team building and customer service and hiring and firing and basket weaving and employee motivation and personal productivity," I wouldn't get a single referral from anybody.

Because if I do all that, I don't do anything well, and I'm threatening all the sales and marketing and leadership and team building and customer service and hiring and firing and basket weaving and employee motivation and personal productivity speakers out there.

So why would anyone refer me? The answer: They wouldn't.

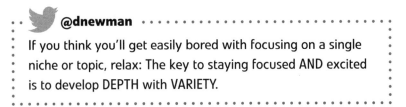

@dnewman

The narrower your focus, the more referable you become.

6. Limitations enhance your creativity and focus.

Instead of shiny object syndrome and going off in a dozen directions at once, consider your niche as the "guardrails" around your business. It keeps you from veering off the path, getting distracted, and going all over the place when what you really want to do is to go a mile deep into your niche, and not spread yourself "a mile wide and an inch deep."

You're going to get a chance to unleash all your innovation, all your creativity, all your great ideas in ONE direction. Breadth will kill you—depth will make you money. And those limitations will totally enhance your creativity and focus and success in the exact area that you want to dominate.

@dnewman

If you think you'll get easily bored with focusing on a single niche or topic, relax: The key to staying focused AND excited is to develop DEPTH with VARIETY.

7. You become the go-to expert in your field.

And once you become so focused and so clear and so deep—guess what?

You're also going to become the go-to expert in your niche. Once you've conquered that first mountaintop that you now clearly OWN, then you'll have plenty of time later to expand and push your elbows out into other adjacent and related areas.

Harsh truth: Even if you ARE great at seventeen different topics, the problem is that from the buyer's perspective, every additional thing you offer diminishes the *perceived expertise* of the original topic they came to you for.

Here are a couple of extra reasons for you because I believe in over-delivering!

8. **You cannot go forward in all directions at once.**

If you want fast, strong, forward movement, you have to go in a single direction. That single direction is going to be determined by your niche.

9. **A niche makes 99 percent of your competition irrelevant.**

If you become the drop-dead, go-to person, 99 percent of the competition falls away and maybe now you have three, four, five competitors total instead of having thousands.

DO IT! SUCCESS STRATEGY: WHAT IS YOUR BIG SEXY IDEA?

BY MARK LEVY

To speak professionally, you need to give the marketplace a reason to choose you over all the other speakers out there. How, though, do you do that?

Use what I call a Big Sexy Idea.

A Big Sexy Idea is your differentiator. It's a differentiating idea that you put at the fore of your speaking business—as the lead concept in your speeches, books, website copy, elevator speech, pitches, and so forth—so you come across to the market as one of a kind.

(continues)

Want examples? All you have to do is play a game of association. Think of a speaker, author, industry expert, or other type of thought leader whose work you admire, and ask yourself what idea comes to mind when you think of them.

If I say "Simon Sinek," you'll likely think . . . "*Start with Why.*"

If I say "Jim Collins," you'll likely think . . . "*Good to Great.*"

If I say "Doris Kearns Goodwin," you'll likely think . . . "Leadership," or perhaps "Leadership lessons from history."

A speaker can of course have many differentiating ideas. For the most part, however, only one idea usually comes to people's minds as dominant.

Take, for instance, Brené Brown. She's written bestsellers like *Daring Greatly*, *Rising Strong*, and *The Gifts of Imperfection*, but when I ask people what idea they associate with her, the majority say "vulnerability" (based on Brown's wildly popular TEDx talk and book *The Power of Vulnerability*).

A critical note: How did these experts tie their name to an impressive idea? It didn't just happen. Instead, they put in the work. Each of them has spoken and written about their idea for years. Their efforts made the idea magic, not the other way around.

With that said, the question becomes: How do you discover an idea that you can make Big and Sexy?

An exercise that's sure to help is one I first learned from my pal Michel Neray. I call it "The Stereotype Exercise." It's in two parts.

Part #1. Stereotypes. Imagine that an audience has come to hear you speak. This audience, however, knows nothing about you, except for one thing: They know your speech topic. That's all. They know you're going to speak about, say, team building. But they don't know anything about your ideas, or philosophy, or stories, or background, or what you're going to recommend.

That said, without knowing you at all, they still have opinions about what they think you're going to say. You might say your audience has stereotypical notions about what they think you're going to say. What kinds of stereotypical notions? I don't know, but you do. Write them down now.

What do people assume you're going to say about your subject?

Part #2. Differences. OK, look over all those preconceived notions you just jotted down. Now, come up with all the ways you're different from the stereotypes.

In other words, what exactly are you going to tell them that's different from what they expect? If you tell people what they already know, they have no reason to listen to you. But if you tell them about a difference, now they have to listen, because they don't know what to expect.

One of your differences may, in fact, be far more important than the others.

By putting in enough work, one of those differences might just make you a headliner.

Mark Levy is the founder of Levy Innovation, a positioning firm that differentiates organizations and thought leaders by using what he calls "a Big Sexy Idea." Mark's clients include Simon Sinek, of Start with Why *fame; CEOs of major brands, like Popeyes; the former head of the Strategy Unit of the Harvard Business School; and the famed cult TV show* Mystery Science Theater 3000. *Mark can be reached at mark@levyinnovation.com.*

20 BE CAREFUL HOW YOU LABEL YOUR SERVICES

Be careful how you label your services. I've seen so many speakers and experts shoot themselves in the foot by not thinking through how to label their services.

Here's what I mean.

Consulting—clients expect to pay top dollar.

Consulting is a premium word. Consulting sounds expensive.

Consulting has historically been positioned as an expensive service.

Coaching—DANGER! You're in the commodity zone.

Be careful with the word "coaching." Coaching sounds like you're the nice HR director who just got laid off, and you had business cards printed at Staples, and you're in between jobs, so now you're a coach, a life coach, a business coach, a this coach, a that coach.

Coaching sounds like a commodity; it sounds cheap.

Before you start sending me hate mail, please understand this has nothing to do with the real, tangible credibility of certified coaches who have done hundreds and hundreds of hours of training or certifying and have letters after their name.

All of that is great, but sadly irrelevant. I'm talking about what most **executives and decisionmakers and buyers** think about when they see the word "coach," and it's this:

Coaching has become commoditized. How can you tell? Because you can't walk into your local chamber's monthly networking event without running into at least three coaches, all of whom sound the same, look the same, and act the same.

Coaching itself, unfortunately, has gotten a bad name. I don't know how it happened or when it started. And I'm not happy about it. I'm just telling you from a marketing, articulation, branding, and positioning standpoint, a consultant is always paid *more* than a coach. A coach is always paid *less* than a consultant. I'm just reporting the news. Don't shoot the messenger!

Training—another word that might make you broke.

Here's another big trap: the word *training*.

Training has also become a devalued term. If a company pays for training, the maximum they'll typically pay is $3,000 or $4,000 a day.

Training becomes a low-level commodity because everyone's doing training. Uncle Bob does training. Seminar companies do training. Your local training franchise does training. Most corporations have an entire training department. Everyone's in the training game. So why do they need you if all you offer is "training"?

You want some better alternatives to the word *training*?

Use the word seminar. Seminar or—even better—"strategic work session"—those are high-end, high-value labels for that same training delivery mode.

You can come in and offer an $8,000-a-day "strategic work session" because you're selling that to an executive. OR you could take that same content and only get $4,000 from a training manager or HR manager, because that is the most they are willing to spend. For that reason, **I suggest you eliminate "training" from your vocabulary when facing the corporate market**.

What do you replace *coaching* with? I don't do coaching. I do either one-on-one consulting or mentoring. For example, I have a ninety-day speaker mentoring program. It runs between $15,000 and $20,000. And every day, people gladly invest.

If I said, "Well, I'll coach you for ninety days." How much is that? People would expect to pay a few hundred dollars per session or maybe a thousand or two per month and I'd be broke.

Whether you call it consulting or coaching or training or seminars or strategic work sessions, there is an economic value that is tied to each of those words. Choose carefully.

I personally don't do any coaching or training.

I do **seminars**. I do **strategic work sessions**.

I don't do any coaching. I do **mentoring** or **one–on–one consulting**.

And I recommend that you do the same.

21 YOU ATTRACT WHAT YOU DEFINE

@dnewman

It's impossible to hit a target that you cannot see.

And it's even more impossible to hit a target that does not exist.

This defining and deciding process is vitally important.

When you define the target, you will vastly increase your chance of hitting the bull's-eye.

Now let me get specific about attracting what you define.

The first definition is around financial outcomes. If you define that you want to have a $100,000 business, that's not going to happen by accident. If you define that you want to create a $500,000 business, that's not going to happen by accident either.

And we're going to talk later in this section about exactly how to work your way backward from the financial outcomes that you want to generate with your speaking-driven business.

If you think about it, you attract what you define in every area of your life, not just financial outcomes. Take work-life balance. You need to define how much you want to work, how much you want to relax, how much vacation time you want to have, and how much time you want to spend with your friends and family and significant other before you can achieve the balance you want to achieve. How much time you spend investing in your business relationships, what kind of business relationships do you want, what level of business relationships do you want?

If you define the perfect prospects, you define what a great consulting project looks like, you define your best-fit coaching clients and speaking audiences, you are going to vastly increase your chance of finding them, connecting with them, and immediately recognizing them when they come across your radar.

And this is going to help you laser-focus on exactly which corporations, associations, conferences, and groups you're going to be the most in demand for, you're going to be the most in sync with, and the best speaking clients who are going to refer, repeat, and recommend you.

Having said all that, I think you'll agree that, when it comes to the definition process, the journey is absolutely worth the trip!

DO IT! SUCCESS STRATEGY: UNLEASH THE POWER OF MASTERMIND GROUPS

BY KARYN GREENSTREET

If it's true that you are a reflection of the five people you spend the most time with, are you surrounding yourself with people who want success as much as you do?

Professional speakers know that none of us is as smart as all of us. We need peers to brainstorm with. Imagine shortening the learning curve and finding solutions to thorny problems by tapping into the know-how and experience of others. This is powerful for your career, and an amazing value to offer your clients and colleagues.

Here's an easy way to get more widely known and increase your revenue: Create paid mastermind groups for your audience around your topic (or build internal groups among your peers at work, or in the professional associations for your industry). Your group will make better strategic decisions and take smarter actions toward their goals.

Jack Canfield, cocreator of the *Chicken Soup for the Soul* series, says, "I don't know anybody who has become super-successful who has not employed the principle of masterminding. If you're not already in a mastermind group, join or start one now."

WHAT IS A MASTERMIND GROUP?

Mastermind groups offer a combination of brainstorming, education, peer accountability, and support. You share best practices, sharpen skills, create savvy goals and action plans, and make wiser decisions.

Members meet regularly and act as catalysts for growth, offering unbiased insights and bringing clarity to fuzzy thinking. To amplify the value of many minds helping each other, the leader brings skillful facilitation and success structures to the group.

WHAT DO YOU GET BY FACILITATING OR PARTICIPATING?

Brainstorming yields answers and ideas. The best part of mastermind groups is that members get immediate help with the challenges that are uppermost in their minds.

Tap into the experience and skill of others. Ongoing education is a must for professionals, but it's hard to find the time to study everything you need to learn. You have access to everyone's knowledge, skills, experience, and best practices.

Accountability and real progress in your professional life. Your mastermind partners help you brainstorm action plans and set up accountability structures that keep you focused and on track.

An instant and valuable support network. You'll gain tremendous insights that improve your business and help you grow as a thought leader. Being a speaker can be lonely with no one to bounce ideas around with—and here is the solution. It's like having an objective board of directors, a success team, and a peer advisory group, all rolled into one.

Regular time to work ON your business or career. Everyday tasks and urgent schedules focus you on working in your business or job. Mastermind groups help you carve out time on a regular basis for thinking strategically about the big picture, and dealing with long-range goal and project planning.

MONETIZE A GROUP OF YOUR OWN

When you're an expert, speaking is just one avenue of revenue open to you. Often speakers create signature programs or workshops as an added stream of income. But your participants want more from you. After they take your class or read your book, how are you going to help them implement all the strategies you've shared? How can they get more help and access from you?

(continues)

Mastermind groups are a huge opportunity for you to expand your reach, leverage your time, and scale your business. Once you learn and master the art of running a group, you can help your members create extraordinary levels of success.

I wouldn't be where I am in business today without the help of my own mastermind group along the way. Isn't it time for you to access this remarkable success tool?

Karyn Greenstreet is the founder of The Success Alliance, a website devoted to helping people start and grow their own mastermind groups. She has been creating and running mastermind groups since 1994, and teaches others to design, fill, and facilitate groups of their own. To learn more about mastermind groups and how you can start one of your own, visit her website at TheSuccessAlliance.com.

22 HOW MUCH MONEY DO YOU WANT TO MAKE?

Here's the financial goal-setting process where the rubber meets the road.

Let's say that you've set out to build a $500,000/year speaking-driven business.

Now let's do that math. Let's figure out how realistic this might be for you. If the speaking fee that you're charging today is $1,000 and you're trying to make $500,000, that means that you would have to deliver 500 gigs over the course of a single year.

Is that doable? Is that practical? Does that make sense? If you have a 1 percent success rate just by using cold calling alone, you would have to make 50,000 phone calls to land 500 gigs. Now making 50,000 phone calls sounds like an awful lot. If there are 220 workdays in the year, that means you're making 227 calls a day. And to deliver 500 programs, you're on the road 365 days a year, sometimes doing 2 gigs in 1 day.

That's just not going to happen. Why? Plain and simple—because the math doesn't work.

As you can see, your $500,000 goal at a $1,000 speaking fee is completely impractical. You have to back into the math the right way.

 **@dnewman**

When it comes to hitting your revenue goals, start with your dream and work backward from there.

That's exactly how this process works. Let's say you want to back into a $300,000/year business. YOU get to decide how busy you want to be and how much money you want to make and how much you need to charge. But as you saw in the example above, the math HAS to work in your favor. If it doesn't, you get to adjust the dials—*lower* the goal, *raise* the fee, or *increase* the work. Once you're dialed in, your financial success becomes much more clearly achievable—and if you get everything else right, perhaps it's *inevitable*!

Let's say you've decided you would like to do one paid keynote speech per month, and the fee you'd like to charge is $7,500.

Make that your first piece of your revenue pie:

Speaking: $7,500 x 12 = $90,000

For your $300,000/year revenue model, you're now almost one-third of the way there.

What are the other investable opportunities in your business?

Maybe you do some one-on-one coaching or consulting. Perhaps you decide that, over the course of the year, you want to get ten one-on-one clients. What do you charge for a one-on-one client? Let's say you have a

Mentor Program that's $15,000. If you get ten clients, that's another $150,000. Now your revenue goal looks like this:

Speaking: $7,500 x 12 = $90,000
Mentoring: $15,000 x 10 = $150,000

You're up to $240,000. What else do you offer? Perhaps you'd like to sell your online course or do group coaching programs. Maybe you offer full-day trainings or strategic work sessions. Perhaps you run CEO round-tables or offer board facilitation or leadership retreats. You might have back-of-the-room products you sell every time you speak. This is all fair game. Remember—YOU get to decide!

To keep this simple, let's say that after you do a keynote for $7,500, a CEO rushes up to you afterward and says, "That was amazing. We have to bring you in to work with our whole executive team." Your full-day strategic work sessions are $10,000. And you like doing them, so your goal is eight of those per year. Here's the final snapshot of your revenue goal:

Speaking: $7,500 x 12 = $90,000
Mentoring: $15,000 x 10 = $150,000
Strategic Work Sessions: $10,000 x 8 = $80,000
TOTAL: $320,000

Here's the best news of all after you've mapped out what you'd like your numbers to look like: This is a MINIMUM goal. Why? Because if you're any good at all with your speaking, you'll get spin-off business from each of those twelve keynotes. If you're mentoring is awesome, you'll get referred and introduced to other executives. If your strategic work sessions are powerful, you'll get repeat and referral business both inside and outside those organizations that you've helped. So it's perfectly reasonable to add another 25 to 40 percent to your baseline revenue goal just from repeat business, referral business, product sales, online course sales, book sales, whatever else you have in your toolkit. Don't count on that—it's gravy. But don't be too surprised if your $320,000 per year becomes a $380,000 per year.

Back when I was mapping all of this out for the first time in my own speaking, consulting, and mentoring business, this is exactly how I started to "back into" my first $300,000 year, then onto $400,000, eventually breaking through the $500,000 barrier and today we run a very healthy multi-seven-figure business built on the same math. The numbers just get bigger!

@dnewman ·

Remember: YOUR math has to work for YOUR business. It's a simple third-grade equation: "Price times quantity equals total."

I meet so many speakers and consultants and experts who just have this fantasy: a random number tied to no math whatsoever. They just have this crazy number in their heads. They have no idea what they need to sell, what their goals are, what their price points need to be, how much they need to sell of any given program or service to meet those goals, and for those reasons, they're flailing and they're guessing and they're winging it.

And then they're wondering, "How come I'm only bringing in $55,000 a year? How come I'm not making six figures? How come I'm not making multiple six figures? Will I ever be able to make a million dollars?"

Well, the answer is yes. You will be able to make a million dollars but not by accident, and not by random, and not by guessing and hoping and praying. But you will be able to make a million dollars if you start with your dream and work backward from there.

DO IT! SUCCESS STRATEGY: QUIT PLAYING THE SHORT GAME AND PLAY THE LONG GAME TO MAKE THE BIG MONEY

BY MARK HUNTER, CSP

Emails to respond to, phone calls to return, deadlines to meet—the race never ends, and the only thing it does is keep you in the short game. As speakers, consultants, and trainers, we know there will never be a time when there are no demands on our time.

The challenge is that the immediate demands on our time keep us playing a short game that never gets us to the long game we need to be playing. If we want to get ahead, we have to play the long game, and it starts with how we focus our time and effort.

First thing we can't forget is there will always be short-term demands on our time. The trick is to take the things we do short term and make them part of our long game.

I work in sales, helping companies and salespeople sell more effectively, and this means having them spend their time with prospects who are in each phase of the selling process. The same is true for us, whether we are a speaker, trainer, or consultant.

Everything we do for an immediate client must be done in a manner that will help us long term. If all we do is focus short term, then all we have is a job. It's when we play the long game that we can say we have a business. The workbook you create or the PowerPoint you build for today's client must fit into your longer-term needs for your business.

Recently, I had to build a two-page document around prospecting for a client presentation. I spent two hours on the document, and yes, it was well received by the client. I then turned that document into four other documents and a video series that fits a long-term objective I have of assets I wanted to create. What I did was take a job I was being paid to do, and with another six hours of work, I turned it into a long-term asset I can reuse in numerous ways. I will now be able to sell it as a stand-alone program, sell it as part of larger client projects, or use portions of it as a lead-magnet.

The example I just shared didn't come by accident. It begins with me having a clear vision of the long game set of objectives I want to achieve and then backing into my short-term activities to see how I can turn each one into a long-term asset.

Before you run out and think you can take every short-term activity and turn it into a long-term asset, I want you to fist ask yourself the question, "What challenge will it help my target market solve?"

Your objective is to now ask yourself that same question before you accept any job, regardless of how good you think it is today. If the short-term job doesn't fit your long-term goals, then you must say NO! This was hard for me to do. The lure of the immediate speaking or training compelled me to accept it, but doing so kept me from turning what I do from a job into a business.

Each day you have to ask yourself, "What will I do today that will move me one step closer to my long-term goal?" Doing that will move you quickly into playing the long game.

Mark Hunter, CSP, "The Sales Hunter," works with salespeople and companies to help them find and retain better prospects. You can find out more by visiting his website at TheSalesHunter.com. To receive his insights weekly, go to thesaleshunter.com/weekly-tips. You can also follow Mark on LinkedIn at linkedin.com/in/markhunter.

23 YOU ARE HERE: THE TURNING POINT

Up to this point, we've been talking about internally focused work—zeroing in on your business model, speaking model, revenue model, messaging, packaging, articulation, distinction.

The moment you first picked up this book, I'm sure some of you felt like, "I'm ready to go, I'm ready to sell, I'm ready to market. Let me get some prospects. Put me in, Coach—let's book some gigs!"

Imagine if you had started marketing and selling and connecting with prospects before you completed all the work in the previous micro-chapters.

No target market.

No niche.

No message. No clarity. No focus.

But still, you were just raring to go. That would have been an absolutely terrible idea and the good news is that this is a pivotal part of the book.

All that came before is designed to help you with your messaging and your packaging and targeting and goals and putting a workable revenue-generating game plan together as an expert who speaks professionally.

This section is the pivot point between our internally focused work and our externally facing sales and marketing and opportunity development campaigns. Those show you everything you need to do as far as tactical targeting, outreach, initializing prospect contact, what to say, how to say it, what to do, how to do it, what to send, how to make the approach, how not to sound like a goofball, and how to build your pipeline and connect with prospects and close some bookings.

 @dnewman

If you don't like the word "sales," you can let that word go. Think of it as opportunity development and you'll master it quickly.

24 YOU WIN THE RACE BY INCHES, NOT MILES

Let's revisit the competitive scan that you did earlier.

As I mentioned, this is both an exhilarating and a depressing exercise because you will realize that there is a LOT of competition out there.

Don't despair because many of those speakers and experts are totally undifferentiated, totally not distinct, totally not special in any way, shape, or form. Too bad they didn't get a copy of this book in their Christmas stocking! (Yes, *Do It! Speaking* books DO make excellent gifts—they freeze well, and they fit every bookshelf.)

Please remember: It takes inches, not miles, to win a race. All you have to be is three inches ahead of the competition to win.

The reason for that is simple:

> 🐦 **@dnewman**
> Your buyers are lazy, busy, and befuddled.

They're not going to do an in-depth analysis and put you in a comparative spreadsheet and do all these calculations. They're going to make a snap judgment in two seconds, five seconds, ten seconds.

That's why you can literally win this race by inches.

That's why you **don't** need to be miles ahead or miles different.

A little twist, a little specialness, a little bit of a unique voice, a little bit of resonance is all it takes. In other words, your message, what you say and how you say it, just needs to resonate with buyers a little bit more . . . and you win.

 **@dnewman**

Your job with every piece of marketing is to convey two and only two ideas to your target prospects: 1. You know what they're going through, and 2. You can fix it.

25 ELEVATE YOUR FEES TO PRO STATUS

Meeting planners, conference producers, association executives, and corporate decisionmakers want to hire true experts—not beginners, dabblers, or amateurs.

Problem is—many speakers position themselves as amateurs by charging fees that are too low and damage their credibility.

From *Smart Meetings* magazine, here's a breakdown of what meeting executives thought of speakers at the following fee levels in their own words:

1. Unpaid: "Mediocre at best, just starting out"
2. $1,000–$2,500: "At this level, you get what you pay for"
3. $2,500–$5,000: "These speakers are in transition from part-time"
4. $5,000–$10,000: "You are hiring a true professional"
5. $10,000+ "*NY Times* bestseller, celebrity, or marquee name"

TIP: **Increase your fees immediately to $4,500 per day or more.** Charge less, and you'll both earn less money AND get hired less often. A bad combination.

Start quoting higher fees and those fees will become a filter for the prospects and clients whom you want to work with.

@dnewman

Premium clients are attracted to premium experts and they expect to pay premium fees.

 **26 LASER-FOCUS YOUR EXPERTISE**

 @dnewman

There's no such thing as a generic solution to a specific problem.

And ALL of our buyers and audiences have specific

problems. If you come across their radar as a "generalist" speaker, expert, or consultant, you'll immediately be passed over as a commodity.

Even when you are hired, it's almost always a price-driven sale and these clients are the hardest to please, the most demanding, and they nitpick, argue, micromanage, and make your life extremely unpleasant.

Once you clarify your expertise, make some decisions, and really hone in on EXACTLY whom you want to serve and EXACTLY what problems you solve, you escape the price-driven sale.

You are now filtering and sorting your prospects and choosing whom you'd like to work with.

No convincing, no persuading.

You made the leap to high-fee expert by offering LESS, not more.

 **@dnewman**

FACT: Specialists get hired more often, more quickly, and at higher fees.

 **27 STOP SMALL POTATOES THINKING/DOING**

What is "small potatoes" thinking? It is settling for speaking at local chambers, libraries, and business organizations filled with broke-ass losers with no overall game plan to target profit-rich niche groups on a national level and build your revenue-generating machine for ALL your investable opportunities, including paid professional speaking, training, consulting, coaching, online courses, retreats, CEO roundtables, high-fee mentor programs, masterminds, etc.

"Small potatoes" thinking leads to some serious problems: no repeatable, reliable marketing process, hit-or-miss execution, weak follow-through with little or no proactive selling, too much distraction—and falling back on reactive "catch-as-catch-can" marketing and taking on random low-fee opportunities as they fall in your lap.

Sometimes, this "small potatoes" syndrome is caused by feeling like "you're just starting out" or you're "not worthy" or you have to "pay your dues" first. This is complete nonsense. And it's wrong.

Reboot your self-image as a national-level expert. Stop marketing locally, where you're "just another consultant," and start marketing and building relationships on a national level, where the fees and opportunities are far greater.

National experts typically quote (and get) fees that are 150 to 500 percent of what their "local yokel" counterparts get.

DO IT! SUCCESS STRATEGY: PRINTING MONEY LEGALLY: LICENSING YOUR INTELLECTUAL PROPERTY TO CORPORATIONS

BY BILL CATES, CSP, CPAE

I have made millions of dollars licensing my intellectual property to corporations of all sizes, all around the world. I'm not telling you this to brag. I'm telling you this in the hopes of inspiring you to do the same.

Without question, licensing my intellectual property is one of the primary reasons I've been able to build and sustain a speaking-related business that generates over $1 million in annual revenue—year after year after year.

My expertise and intellectual property is built around helping professionals and corporations acquire more clients through referrals, introductions from advocates, and developing more compelling value propositions.

Companies pay me money for the right to use my intellectual property to train their sales force (reps and managers). My first licensing deal was with Mutual of Omaha in 1999. They wanted to find a way to get my system into the hands of their reps and managers that was both affordable and efficient (to get everyone trained in a relatively short period of time).

We decided that creating a series of video lessons would be best. In this program for Mutual of Omaha, and almost all my other licens-

(continues)

STOP SMALL POTATOES THINKING/DOING

ing programs since, a facilitator would deliver the training by playing the video lessons—starting and stopping at predetermined points to hold discussion or to practice skills. I developed a detailed facilitator's guide that made this a very turnkey process.

The beauty of this agreement with Mutual of Omaha was that they didn't want their brand on the training. They wanted it to "come from the outside." Therefore, our agreement also stated that I was the sole owner of the content (critically important) and that I was free to sell the training program to anyone else. I was also lucky in that this client put their video production capabilities at my disposal. In exchange for their video production assistance, I applied a discount toward their licensing fee.

My first video-based training program was delivered via VHS tape. After a few years, we migrated the system onto DVD. Now, all of my video-based training is internet-based. While some folks in our business will create train-the-trainer programs, where the corporate trainers deliver the program, I've opted to have all of my training delivered through video, and led by a facilitator. This allows for a more uniform training experience.

PRICING YOUR LICENSING PROGRAM

When it comes to deciding what to charge for your licensing program, it's still the Wild Wild West. There are no rules or guidelines. It boils down to what the client is willing to invest in your training. Generally speaking, the hierarchy of how much corporations will invest in training their employees—from higher to lower—is: (1) leaders, (2) managers, (3) sales reps, (4) customer service reps, (5) support staff.

If you can draw a straight line to dollars—making money or saving money—you can usually charge more.

PRINTING MONEY LEGALLY

Why do I call this revenue stream "printing money legally"? It's simple. I have a number of licensing deals that are now into their fourteenth year. Each year, when it's time to renew the agreement, I simply change the date in the renewal agreement and send it over with an invoice. My cost of sale is virtually zero dollars.

Bill Cates, CSP, CPAE, is a founding member of the National Speakers Association's Million Dollar Speakers Group. He was inducted into the Professional Speakers Hall of Fame in 2010. He can be reached at: BillCates@ReferralCoach.com or on the web at ReferralCoach.com.

 # 28 PROFESSIONALIZE YOUR SELLING

Five-figure speakers typically lack a target market focus and sometimes don't even know who their most relevant buyers are. It is very hard to hit a target that you cannot see.

What you need is a far more effective and efficient approach that involves finding specific decisionmakers at specific corporations, associations, and groups using your new laser-focused value prop. High relevance. High value. High fee.

How? Create what I call an "Active 20" prospect list.

These are twenty specific buyers at twenty specific organizations that you want to speak for or work with. You actively reach out to them.

You find them via Google, LinkedIn, industry databases, strategic introductions, referrals, and then you connect with them in a high-trust, high-touch campaign. Not to sell them. But to serve them in a well-organized multistep relationship-building sales campaign.

Spend an afternoon researching to find twenty specific decisionmakers at twenty target organizations you'd like to "hire" as your next client. Map out a campaign where you can offer value and invite engagement. Track your progress.

Moving away from a reactive, random sales process to a proactive, highly targeted sales system can double your selling power almost overnight.

 # 29 INTERVIEWS AS A PROSPECTING STRATEGY

How do you know what your prospects and buyers really want and need?

First tip: Don't guess. Don't hope. Don't wing it!

Do some research. If you're evaluating several different potential niche markets or vertical industries, spend some time on researching each one.

Live in their world, think about their problems, and think about their clients and prospects. What's the first step? Data gathering. Preparation. Homework. Industry, regional, business, and company news is now at everyone's fingertips on the internet. Look for articles, blogs, verbatim quotes from executives and industry analysts, video clips, audio interviews, and capture as much as you can.

Then go directly to the source—real live customers and prospects.

Here is a simple, repeatable process for researching what types of speaking services and programs your target market will pay for—and use this strategy to start prospecting tomorrow.

This is GOLD—and it's also one of the easiest and most enjoyable ways you can prospect, build relationships, and break down barriers to high-level decisionmakers who might otherwise be unreachable.

Yes. It's. That. Good.

Forget that you're a speaker. As of right now, you're a writer, researcher, journalist.

Find the top trade association magazines or industry publications that your target executives read, recognize, and respect. And prepare to write an article for them.

Why? Because thought leaders do original research . . .

For prospecting purposes, this is priceless.

* You access high-level buyers it would take you months to reach (if ever!).
* You establish yourself as an expert and a peer.
* You have a good reason for a series of follow-up relationship-building opportunities.

First step: The title of your article series must contain an embedded compliment.

For example, "How Smart Leaders at Top Companies Profit from Breakthrough Innovations" (for an innovation speaker, for example).

Or "How Top Producers at Leading Firms Create Referrals for Life" (for a sales speaker focused on financial services firms).

Ask three to six questions, such as

* What's been the biggest factor in your success?
* What obstacles and challenges are you still working on?
* What's the best advice you've ever heard on this topic?
* In your opinion, what's the secret sauce that many miss?
* What's the key practice or tactic you keep coming back to?
* Crystal ball: What does YOUR next level of success look like in this arena?

Do these by phone or video, whichever they prefer (video is better for rapport).

Map out your approach and all follow-up touchpoints over the next ninety days:

Interview—thank-you email—thank-you card—send finished piece—send link to blog—offer to stop by and drop off signed copy of your book—send different article—invite them to seminar—send note "another idea for you"—Call and say, "I was thinking about your situation" and ask if they would value a conversation about how you might help.

Do three of these per week and you'll get twelve per month. That means that, in ninety days, you'd have thirty-six top prospects who know your name, will take your call, and who might even look forward to hearing from you!

One speaker who wanted to do a lot more work with associations did a series of interviews with association executive directors and conference producers under the banner of "The Association Speaker of Tomorrow"—guess what happened?

He used that information to BECOME the association speaker they wanted to hire!

Another client I worked with wanted to go deep into banks and credit unions. He used my interview strategy, and within a few short weeks, he landed interviews with a dozen CEOs including those of the second- and third-largest credit unions in the nation plus the CEO of every major community bank in his home state of Arkansas. From these interviews and following my advice, he landed a regular column in TWO major credit union industry publications. From the follow-up he's doing, he's building great relationships with these CEOs on a first-name basis and they're looking forward to hearing from him.

30 THE ONLY THREE PROBLEMS YOU CAN SOLVE

You may deliver the world's greatest speech, or the most stellar executive coaching program, or a truly world-class consulting package . . .

You may have trademarked the most amazing methodology or model that your industry has ever seen . . .

Your flagship service may be the most effective on the planet with the ONLY 100 percent bulletproof money-back guarantee in the business . . .

 @dnewman

> Harsh truth: No prospect has a speaker problem. They don't have a methodology deficiency. They don't stay up at night wishing for a new consultant. All they care about is RESULTS.

Almost ALL of your prospects WILL have business problems.

There are only three business problems that you, as a speaker, trainer, consultant, or expert, are ever going to be in a position to solve.

And solving these three specifically, quickly, and profitably is your MAIN and ONLY job—assuming you want to make the greatest contribution to your clients and truly serve them in a way that translates to their bottom line so that they want to pay you enormous amounts of money.

Would you like to know what these three business problems are?

Sure you would—so the next three modules lay out **your new mission, your new mantra, and your new focus**.

Let's say you're about to sit down with a corporate decisionmaker.

A top executive (maybe the CEO, maybe a senior VP—but definitely someone with an executive position AND check-writing authority for what you market and sell).

Depending on the size of the company, you might want to start with one or more questions like these:

* "You have a whole portfolio of products and services and programs. What are the two or three top drivers as you see them?" (Note: CEOs love this kind of talk!)
* "And what are the two or three initiatives that you're putting a lot of resources behind that absolutely have to be successful for you to look back on this year as a banner year?"
* "Imagine you have a whole dashboard—which two or three needles are you looking to move?"

Once they lay out their situation and you've asked a few follow-up questions to flesh out their answers, ask a question like, "Based on everything that you can see from where you're sitting [a nice nod to their power that suggests they're sitting on their throne!], what are two or three of the biggest obstacles in your way?"

They may answer you right away or they might ask you for clarification, at which point you bring out the big guns and say, "Well, typically, we're brought in when people in your position are up against one or more of these three problems: People problems, Process problems, and Profit problems. Which is the most relevant one for you?"

Some good follow-up questions include:

* Where are your competitors biting at your heels?
* In what areas are you winning today and want to move even further ahead?
* What are some internal challenges?
* How do your good ideas sometimes get derailed?
* What are the black holes in your organization (where ideas/projects go to die)?
* What are some process problems?
* Where would you like to grease the wheels and get things rolling more smoothly?

Once you have the basics of the situation in hand, you can then begin to work in the three Ps sales conversation centering around **People, Process,** and **Profit**.

Let's dig into People problems first . . .

DO IT! SUCCESS STRATEGY: NEVER, EVER GIVE THE SAME SPEECH TWICE

BY SAM RICHTER, CSP

I'm going to let you in on a key secret to speaking success. You don't have to be the most engaging storyteller. You don't have to have the flashiest PowerPoint presentations. You don't need to create interactive audience participation exercises. Yes . . . those items are all important, especially for those wishing to make professional speaking their career.

Yet as someone who has attended thousands of conferences and thus heard thousands of speakers, the little-known secret guaranteed to get you a positive review, and, most important, ensure the audience understands and even embraces your message is actually quite simple, yet it is far too often overlooked: customized relevance.

Said another way, "customized relevance" is doing your homework and tailoring your stories and examples to what the audience cares about.

People attend your presentation because they are interested in your expertise and what you have to say. At least that's what you think.

However, the real reason your audience is spending their valuable time with you is they want to know how your message will impact their lives. How will your message help them achieve their personal

(continues)

and/or business goals a little more efficiently, a little more effectively, and/or a little more profitably than they might be able to do on their own?

Following are some techniques to help you quickly find information, so you can customize your examples and stories:

Trends Search: Speaking at a financial services conference? The last thing your audience wants to know about is how your brilliant techniques helped someone in the cosmetics industry. Yet if you understand the trends and issues that your financial services audience is facing, you can customize your cosmetics story and get right to the heart of what your audience cares about.

To find relevant industry trends, conduct a Google search like this: "financial services" + (trends OR issues). On the results page, look for the Tools tab under the search form. Click on it, choose the Any Time pull down, and select Past Year. In seconds you will find information related to current trends and issues in financial services. Under the search form, click the News tab to find news articles related to financial services trends. Click back to the regular search results and add *filetype:pdf* OR *filetype:ppt* to your search. This will deliver white papers, research reports, and other presentations featuring relevant information and data.

News Search: Speaking at a company conference? Find out what's going on in their world, right now, and relate an example or story to their situation. Speaking at an industry conference? Ask for the names of some attendee companies and research the organizations prior to your presentation and feature the companies' accomplishments in your program (hint: You can make a great impression by using the companies of the people on the committee who hired you).

To find the latest company news, go to yougotthenews.com. In the Name field, enter the company name (no need to put within quotation marks as YGTN will do that automatically) or even the executive's name who is in attendance. In the date field, put the current year. On the results page, click the various tabs to find relevant news items; start with the Press Releases tab as that tells you what the company cares about.

Power Search: Consider a subscription to the Sales Intel Engine at sellingintel.com. Not only is this one of the most powerful sales preparation tools around, you can use the various features to almost instantly implement what is described above. In seconds you can search for information on companies, people, and, in the Documents section, find the latest information on industry trends, research, and more just by typing a term or two into one of the fields. The Intel Engine literally can decrease the amount of time you spend researching from hours or days down to minutes or even seconds.

Secret Shop/Call: Speaker extraordinaire Ross Bernstein (www .rossbernstein.com) uses this technique to perfection, consistently resulting in standing ovations and invitations for repeat programs. Get the names of companies in attendance and visit or call a few of those businesses prior to your presentation. Pretend you're a real customer. Interact with people at the organization looking for good examples of how people in your attendees' organizations already practice what you preach.

In your presentation, ask the person in the audience from that company—it will typically be an executive—to stand up. Then share the story of your amazing experience and you will see the individual beam with pride. Make audience members the heroes of your stories and it doesn't matter if you stumble on a few words or your Power-Points aren't the fanciest because everyone in the audience will take your message to heart, and you will show that you truly care about them. And you will completely differentiate yourself from probably every other speaker at the conference.

Take the time to research your attendees. Learn what they care about. Customize your stories and examples to their industry. Make your audience members the hero. Yes, it takes extra time versus

(continues)

showing up with your canned PowerPoint and canned speech. Yet the time invested customizing your presentation with relevant information and stories will take your personal brand and reputation to a new and highly respected level.

Sam Richter, CSP, is considered one of the world's foremost experts on sales intelligence and digital reputation management. Through his in-person keynote presentations and his online learning programs and resources, Sam annually entertains tens of thousands of executives and helps leading organizations around the globe generate millions of dollars in new business through relevant information. Learn more at SamRichter.com.

 # 31 YOU SOLVE PEOPLE PROBLEMS

As you're leading the sales conversation with your prospect, you can talk specifically about people obstacles (not people individually but their "people issues" as obstacles) because you want to get the lay of the land to understand what they're up against.

People problems come in all shapes and sizes, but here's a starter list so you can ask more intelligently about them with your prospects:

* Arrogance
* Coaching
* Collaboration
* Communication
* Complacency
* Delegation

- ✳ Employee engagement
- ✳ Entitlement
- ✳ Gossip, gab, and the grapevine
- ✳ Leadership
- ✳ Micromanagement
- ✳ Negativity
- ✳ Perfectionism
- ✳ Recognition and reward
- ✳ Recruiting top talent
- ✳ Retention of top talent
- ✳ Silos and turf wars
- ✳ Staff utilization
- ✳ Succession
- ✳ Teamwork

No matter what your speaking, training, coaching, or consulting focus might be—they can ALL be tied to solving one or more of these underlying people problems, risks, or gaps.

Yes, really.

In fact, if you're not talking about these, you're positioning yourself as a "nice-to-have" and NOT as a "must-have."

Decisionmakers ALWAYS need to solve SOME of the above problems and make improvements in the rest of them. They do NOT always "need" to hire a speaker, trainer, or expert.

Tie them TOGETHER—and you win.

32 YOU SOLVE PROCESS PROBLEMS

Process problems show up as inefficiencies, gaps,

missed opportunities, too much wasted time or effort, too many steps, too much bureaucracy or paperwork or too many layers between customer and company.

There are entire industries built around business process improvement, and a handful of fads from the 1950s to the 1990s didn't help—the total quality movement, business process reengineering, outsourcing, insourcing, rightsizing, you name it.

Let's cut to the chase and catalog a brief list of potential sources of process problems that you may want to discuss with your prospect in order to get their attention focused on the desired OUTCOME of investing in your speeches, seminars, or consulting.

* Accounting
* Billing
* Call centers
* Contracting
* Customer service
* Delivery
* Distribution
* Engineering
* Facility management
* Finance
* Hiring
* Information systems
* Innovation
* Inventory management
* Manufacturing
* Marketing

* Operations
* Payroll
* Product development
* Recruiting
* Regulatory compliance
* Research and development
* Sales
* Strategic planning
* Workforce diversity

Tie some of these into your sales conversations and, again, you win!

 # 33 YOU SOLVE PROFIT PROBLEMS

Profit problems come in many shapes and sizes.

What's important is that when you are marketing and selling your speaking services that you do NOT overlook this vitally important problem that is NEVER far from the mind of any serious decisionmaker.

 @dnewman

If profitability is NOT a big deal to your prospect, then you are talking to the wrong prospect!

Often placed at the end of a chain reaction of internal and external variables (where your speaking, coaching, or consulting comes into play), when you talk about solving your customers' profitability problems, the outcomes almost always end up with YOU using the following "so that" phrases:

* So that you sell more often . . .
* So that you sell at full price . . .
* So that you avoid discounting . . .
* So that you open new markets . . .
* So that you expand your product line . . .
* So that you cut costs . . .
* So that you manufacture and distribute more efficiently . . .
* So that you speed up time to market . . .
* So that you cross-sell . . .
* So that you upsell . . .
* So that you open new channels . . .
* So that you raise prices . . .
* So that you boost your margins . . .
* So that your per unit cost goes down . . .
* So that you franchise . . .
* So that you license . . .
* So that your stock price goes up . . .
* So that you conserve more cash . . .

Spoiler alert: If your focus is on solving **people problems**, you may have been saddened to see all the process and profit problems just now. Here's the secret . . .

One hundred percent of these problems are PEOPLE problems in disguise.

Why? Because someone owns the screwed-up process and hasn't fixed it. Someone else owns the unprofitable business unit, product, or division—and they cannot or will not face the problem, deal with the consequences, and fix it. So if you solve people problems, you can have a marketing conversation on ALL of these levels and **you get three chances to make your case!**

34 WHY HIRE YOU?

How can your expertise become *congruent* with the priorities of your prospects?

And how do you separate yourself from the crowd and stand out from the pack if they're considering multiple different speakers or experts?

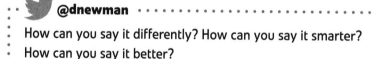

@dnewman

How can you say it differently? How can you say it smarter? How can you say it better?

How can you say it with a twist that's unique to you and your voice and your value proposition?

To prove in a brief document that you are different and not the same as everyone else, create a "Why Hire You" document.

The seven consistent themes that meeting planners, conference producers, and association executives say they want in their speakers are:

1. **Expertise**—REAL in-depth knowledge, specifics, actionable takeaways, templates, tools, scripts—not theory or fluff.
2. **Currency**—Up-to-the-minute, current, and cutting-edge information, ideas, and insights.
3. **Relevance**—Directly relevant stories, examples, and case studies that are industry specific. Tailoring and personalization is no longer optional.
4. **Easy to work with**—Don't be a jerk. Be responsive. Be fun.
5. **Interaction**—No talking heads or lectures. Mix things up. Use activities, conversation, and interaction to get the audience to tap into each other.
6. **Experience**—Buyers want to hear from people who have DONE things in the real world. There's a premium on experience and accomplishments. You probably have them—but aren't talking about them. Tap into your "real" work experience BEFORE you became speaker.
7. **Authenticity**—Buyers want to see the real you. Not a pompous jerk reading a PowerPoint. So the more you can keep it real, the better. The more you can relate to the audience and connect with them, the better. The more you can share both your mistakes and your successes, the better.

What stories can you tell, what indisputable points of proof can you point to, what factual data can you share in your "Why Hire You" document to demonstrate each of these seven points?

To see some great examples of "Why Hire You" sheets, visit www.doit marketing.com/speak to grab the companion resources and downloads. You'll find several completed examples and a blank template for you to create your own "Why Hire You" sheet.

DO IT! SUCCESS STRATEGY: HOW TO BUILD AN ICONIC REPUTATION AS A SPEAKER

BY SCOTT MCKAIN, CSP, CPAE

"You should know," the successful CEO informed the owner of the renowned speakers bureau, "I always receive a terrific response from the audiences at my presentations."

"That's great," the bureau owner replied. "Who is in the audience?"

The CEO answered exactly as the bureau owner believed he might: "It's the employees of our company."

"I'm not interested," the bureau owner surprisingly responded, "until I see video of you speaking to people who don't have your name on their paycheck."

The primary test is not how a speaker's ideas captivate those predisposed to respond favorably. Instead it is how to enthrall an audience entering an event tired, bored, pissed off, and uncommitted to the ideas about to be espoused.

Given the reticence of response that professional speakers frequently face, how does one carve out an iconic presence in the marketplace?

There are five factors of iconic performance:

* **Play Offense**
* **Stop Selling**
* **Go Negative**
* **Get Promise vs. Performance Right**
* **Reciprocal Respect**

Play Offense: Know your competition—but don't make them the focus of your efforts. Research demonstrates defense does *not* win championships. It's great to know the work of other presenters. You

(continues)

87

should learn what other speakers deliver, but it cannot be the basis of your efforts. You must create your own work, your own material, your own style, your own presentation. Take the offensive and make the platform yours. We already have a Tony Robbins. What we need is you.

Stop Selling: This does NOT mean that you shouldn't market your services. It does mean that the best speakers do not feel the need to always be hawking their programs. How can I possibly believe that you're the right presenter for my event if you are always desperately selling me? We're tired of speakers who are twisting our arms and manipulating us to buy their wares. Stop selling me. Offer value first—which attracts me to want more from you.

Go Negative: This doesn't suggest you should have a negative attitude. It means the only way you'll grow as a speaker is to get coaching that will reveal where you can improve. A true mentor or coach will tear down what you're doing—AND build up your potential to the highest. If you fear the negative, you'll never fully embrace your power on the platform.

Get Promise vs. Performance Right: In desperation to secure bookings, some speakers promise and present the most outlandish claims. "World's #1 All-Time Sales Speaker," one said. The problem was, it wasn't Zig Ziglar—it was someone I'd never heard of. "#1 Keynoter on Customer Service" read another. When I asked the speaker where he had attained that level of recognition, he sheepishly explained he was on a small program with two others on customer service—and, of the three, he ranked at the top. That's deceptive marketing. Once, I had a reporter ask how I could prove my promise that I was a "bestselling author." I presented the royalty receipts from my literary agent, clearly confirming my status. Could your promises pass the same degree of scrutiny about your level of performance?

Finally, **Reciprocal Respect:** Some speakers are prima donnas—insisting the audience respect them more than they display an equivalent level of esteem for the group. Conversely, I've also seen beginners who are intimidated by the event and have such exceeding admiration for the audience, they fail to deliver a high level of performance. Neither is correct. When you respect the audience equal to the level that you can rightfully expect in return, you create a congruent bond with your listeners that is essential for a successful presentation.

Combining these five factors into your efforts to develop an iconic reputation as a speaker can help you market, maximize, and monetize your personal brand.

Scott McKain, CSP, CPAE, is a globally recognized authority who helps organizations and leaders attain the highest level of distinction in the marketplace. A member of the Sales & Marketing Hall of Fame and the Professional Speakers Hall of Fame, his latest book is ICONIC. *For more information, visit ScottMcKain.com.*

35 IF YOU WRITE THE TEST, YOU GET AN "A"

Another great way to dominate your marketplace as a speaker, consultant, or mentor is to prepare a document that lists the twenty questions clients should ask before hiring someone like you.

If you're a leadership speaker, yours will be "20 Questions to Ask Before Hiring Any Leadership Speaker." If you're a social media consultant, "20 Questions to Ask Before Hiring Any Social Media Consultant." If you run a team-building company, "20 Questions to Ask Before Hiring Any Team-Building Company." Here's the secret, folks: **If you write the test, you're going to get an A.**

If you write the test so that YOU have all the right answers, you're going to set the buying criteria for your prospects. This makes their decision easier, so you're truly helping them, and it makes YOU the standout obvious choice, so you're helping yourself at the same time.

Invest the time to write these twenty questions and send them to prospects early in the prospecting discussion. Because there's no better way to start a relationship than a conversation like this:

YOU: Are you looking at a couple of different speakers right now?
PROSPECT: Yes we are.

YOU: Great. Let me send you a document that will help you make a good decision whether it's with me or not.

Here are some sample questions to get you started:

* Does the speaker customize real content or just title pages?
* Does their topic directly tie in to your audience's core issues?
* Is the speaker entertaining as well as informative?
* Does the speaker provide handout masters at no extra charge?
* Does the speaker involve and engage the audience? How?
* Does the speaker use only clean language and humor?

When you send this to a decisionmaker, it sparks a little bit of panic in their mind. They start to think, *"Oh my gosh, I didn't ask that last speaker this question and it seems kind of important."* Who has their answer right under the buyer's nose? YOU DO!

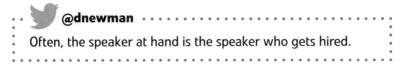
@dnewman
Often, the speaker at hand is the speaker who gets hired.

Because you wrote the questions to help them make their buying decision, you're automatically positioning yourself as the number one choice and now any other speakers they're considering are being vetted against YOUR criteria.

I'll stretch your thinking even further on this one: Your job is **not** to get hired as a speaker; your job is to help your buyer make the safest possible speaker-hiring decision.

MAKE yourself the safest choice and watch how many new doors open for you when you knock!

Bonus tip: You can create a "20 Questions" document not only for your speaking—but also for your consulting or mentoring or facilitation services.

For example, here's the "20 Questions" sheet that we share to help our prospects make a smart decision about joining the Speaker Profit Formula mentorship program:

20 Questions to Ask Before Enrolling with ANY Speaker Marketing Coach/Mentor

To get a printable "20 Questions" template, visit doitmarketing.com/speak.

Compare Company			
A	B	C	The Questions to Ask
——	——	——	1. Does the company specialize in working with speakers and experts?
——	——	——	2. Is the mentoring format designed to suit varied learning styles?
——	——	——	3. Is there an exclusive focus on application and "do-this-now" steps?
——	——	——	4. Does the training include built-in follow-up and accountability?
——	——	——	5. Does the mentoring tie in to YOUR exact business issues?
——	——	——	6. Is there an online component to the training available 24/7?
——	——	——	7. Will I learn situational strategies in addition to personal skills?

Compare Company			
A	B	C	The Questions to Ask (continued)
——	——	——	8. Is the program relevant to ALL levels of speakers and experts?
——	——	——	9. Is there a *specialist* team to help you, not just a single mentor?
——	——	——	10. Will I be intellectually stimulated enough to feel challenged?
——	——	——	11. How current/fresh is the content that I will be learning?
——	——	——	12. Will I get a complete library of templates, tools, and scripts?
——	——	——	13. Will I be learning from a proven, published, and certified speaker?
——	——	——	14. Does the mentor have LOTS of verifiable client success stories?
——	——	——	15. Do I have access to an ongoing source of support between calls?
——	——	——	16. Will I get some done-for-you services, not just coaching alone?
——	——	——	17. Will there be NO hidden charges or fees once I enroll?
——	——	——	18. Has the mentor been coaching other speakers for a LONG time?
——	——	——	19. Is the mentor just a *bored speaker* OR a *full-time business coach*?
——	——	——	20. Does the company qualify clients (or will they work with anyone)?
——	——	——	Score

36 SPEAKER WEBSITE RULE #1

Let's talk about rules of the road for professional speaker websites. What are the must-haves and what are the nice-to-haves and what are the don't-even-worry-about-its?

Rule number 1 is to share content. I know this seems intuitively obvious, but some speakers still don't get it.

Here's what I mean by sharing content. You need to have a **resource–rich website** that demonstrates your thinking.

Some people would argue that no one pays a professional *speaker* BUT they happily pay a professional *thinker* to come in and speak.

If you're a professional thinker that means that you've got articles, you've got downloads, you've got value items that share your credibility and that outline the same kinds of ideas, strategies, tactics, and tools that you would share with your clients and audiences.

BS Warning: You'll hear other "speaker gurus" preach that if you're going to present yourself as a serious professional speaker, you absolutely have to have a book.

Question: Are you going to delay your entire speaking career for six months or a year or two years until you write and finish and publish a book?

Of course not. Here's my take on this:

 @dnewman

If you have a book, that's great. If you don't have a book, you don't need a book to be a speaker. All you need are tangible sources of excellence.

Buyers want to put their hands on your tangible sources of excellence. You can't be out there saying, "I'm a speaker. I'm really smart. I've got a great message. Trust me."

It's not "trust me"—it's **show me**.
And your "show me" strategy relies on sharing top-notch content.

* There are $15,000 speakers who don't have a book—but they have a Top 50 podcast on iTunes and that's their tangible source of excellence.
* There are $15,000 speakers who don't have a book—but they write top-notch content on their blog and that's their tangible source of excellence.
* There are $15,000 speakers who don't have a book—but they have a terrific YouTube channel with hundreds of thousands of views and that's their tangible source of excellence.
* There are $15,000 speakers who don't have a book—but they regularly publish in their industry's top trade journals, association magazines, and industry publications and that's their tangible source of excellence.
* There are $15,000 speakers who don't have a book—but they host the market-leading livestream or conference or LinkedIn or Facebook community for their industry and that's their tangible source of excellence.

Why is it important to share your great content and make it obvious that you have lots more where that came from?

It used to be that in the good old days, twenty years ago when dinosaurs roamed the convention centers, the typical speaker spiel was, "I'm a great speaker. I do a great speech. You should bring me in. You should hear the speech. Hoo boy—this speech is awesome."

@dnewman
Today, it's about expertise. It used to be that clients hired speakers. Now they hire smart people who speak.

When I was a conference producer and a meeting planner myself, I would often connect with speakers and I would ask, "Hey, where's that article, where's that PDF, where's that philosophy that you just talked about?" and they would say, "Oh, that's not on my website. I don't put that out there. That's not an article—I couldn't share that with you because that's *my stuff*. That's what I get paid the big bucks for."

And I would laugh. I'd say, "You know what? I'm not going to pay you any bucks if I can't see the tangible sources of excellence and if I can't understand the ideas, philosophies, strategies, tactics, and methodology that you're going to share with my group."

Meeting planners are not going to *hope*. They're not going to *guess*. They're not going to *pray*. They need to see proof. And if you don't have proof on your website, they're going to move on and hire the next speaker who does.

 @dnewman

Don't be stingy with your content unless you want buyers to be stingy with your fee.

DO IT! SUCCESS STRATEGY: AUTHENTICALLY SOCIAL: PUT COMMUNITY & CONNECTION AT THE CORE OF YOUR DIGITAL STRATEGY

BY COREY PERLMAN

Gone are the days of questioning whether social media is an effective marketing strategy. We've either seen success ourselves or watched as others have created awareness, stayed "top of mind," or increased leads. But with every successful social media success story, there are many others flailing about, wondering why they can't move the proverbial needle. I've pondered this question over the last few years and believe that we have officially swung from one end of the pendulum all the way to the other.

(continues)

Twitter is my favorite example of this massive swing. When it first launched, it was this massive platform of people connecting with people. Today, it's dominated by bots, automated direct messages, and prepopulated content. There's very little authentic about it anymore. And thus, it's lost its luster.

And it's happening on all social platforms. LinkedIn has become a spammers paradise and Facebook is filled with brands putting out automated content hoping to stay on the radar of potential prospects. The key word that has been lost on all of these sites is . . . SOCIAL.

So . . . let's talk about you. If I check out your digital footprint, what will I see? Is it made up of a mix of engaging content that is worthy of your fans and followers? Or is it a sea of curated content with no connection to your identity? Would you consider yourself to be authentically social?

Here are a few questions I want you to think about:

1. What's your unique identity? What makes you, your content, or your presentation different than your competition?

2. What's your unique value proposition? How does your expertise benefit others?

3. How would you define your style? Quick and witty? Powerful and passionate? Dry and sarcastic? Why do people enjoy listening to you?

4. How can you consistently produce digital content that brings your above answers to life?

Here are a few examples of how you might make your content more authentically social:

1. Bring people behind the scenes at your events. Provide a glimpse inside the world of a professional

speaker and how your preparation techniques or travel tips might be of benefit to them.

2. Do a series of episodes using Facebook or Instagram live. Answer questions, discuss current topics, or share excerpts from your latest book.

3. Incorporate your family life into your personal brand. I take my daughter on work trips with me all the time and my tribe enjoys seeing the mix of me being a professional speaker and a dad!

4. Use your network to do a series of interviews with influencers in your industry. This can be done via video, podcast, or as an article. You get to shine a spotlight on professionals in your network and add value to the rest of your tribe at the same time!

If you've come to the realization that your digital footprint can become more authentically social, then I encourage you to take small steps to improve. Take one idea from above (or something else that you come up with) and implement it on a consistent basis. Make it routine. One consistent, episodic video series that you produce on Facebook or Instagram (or both!) can make a world of difference. It can bring your brand to life and help you get noticed on the biggest social platforms in the world.

Here are a couple of friendly reminders before you embark on this new initiative to become more authentically social:

* Be consistent. One episode, video, or Instagram story won't do much for you. It's the sum of a consistent series that will make the difference. Stay the course; people will eventually take notice.

(continues)

* Brainstorm. The best ideas will come from within. In your next team meeting, bring this topic up and see what ideas come from the team. No one knows your industry or what matters to your tribe better than you and your team.

* Engage with your own stuff! Remind the team to get on Facebook and Instagram and engage! Likes, comments, and shares tend to happen in bunches so give your content a nice start by getting friends, family, and colleagues to individually promote.

* Call to action. This doesn't need to be overly aggressive, but remind people how to contact you, get to your site, or come see you. At the end of the day, we are a business and so it's important to connect the dots from social follower to happy client!

Corey Perlman is a speaker, consultant, and nationally recognized social media expert. He's the author of two bestselling books, eBoot Camp *and* Social Media Overload! *As the president and founder of Impact Social Inc., Perlman and his team provide social media consulting services to businesses and brands around the globe. For more info, visit ImpactSocial Media.com or CoreyPerlman.com.*

37 SPEAKER WEBSITE RULE #2

Rule number 2 for speaker websites is to put your **phone number and email address everywhere**.

Do not make people hunt. Do not make people look. Make it easy.

Someone once said that people surf the web like monkeys on crack. You have to give them the banana, otherwise they leave. What's the one thing that they can do right now in a single click to consume your content, watch your video, engage with you as an expert?

If they want to call you, put your phone number *everywhere*. Put it up in your website header. Bake it into your header graphic. The phone number's literally on every single page of your website. There should also be a link to your email address in the header or footer of every single page.

 **@dnewman**
Make yourself easy to find, easy to contact, and easy to book.

How many leads are you prepared to lose? They *were* interested but there wasn't an easy-to-find phone number. Boom—they're gone! What's your speaking fee? That's how much money you lost just now.

Now some speakers think, "I'm good. My phone number's on my contact page. If they want to contact me, they should go to my contact page."

When speakers tell me that, I say that's nice. Are you willing to bet $5,000 or $7,500 or $10,000 that they are going to go to your contact page? I wouldn't—and neither should you.

38 SPEAKER WEBSITE RULE #3

The third rule for speaker websites is to **give visitors a reason to come back, a reason to sign up, a reason to opt in.**

Everybody who lands on your website (an audience member, meeting planner, conference producer, corporate executive, training manager, new website visitor)—every single person who visits your website—and **does not** give you their email address is a lost opportunity: lost opportunity for a sale, lost opportunity for a speech, lost opportunity for a referral, lost opportunity for an introduction.

You want to have multiple ways to intrigue them, entice them, and to invite them to leave their email address with you. It's both a list-building strategy and a trust-building strategy.

Whether it's watching your free web training, downloading something, subscribing to something, getting a tip, getting a PDF, getting a free video series, cheat sheet, checklist, or manifesto . . . get their email by making it irresistible.

 **@dnewman**

On your speaker website, encourage, invite, and seduce visitors to not just look around, but to come in, sit down, and get comfortable.

And the best and most valuable deposit they can make to your bank account on their first visit is their email address. If you don't have a mechanism for doing that, sit down with your web designer and ask, "What can we do today, this week, to increase our opt-ins, increase our list building, make this more seductive and more attractive and more effective for capturing email addresses?"

Want some examples? Sure you do—so here you go:

doitmarketing.com/webinar (free training for speakers)

doitmarketing.com/manifesto (thirty-five-page manifesto based on my first book)

doitmarketing.com/podcast (top-rated podcast for experts who speak)

doitmarketing.com/sell ("Sell More Speaking" master-class webinar)

doitmarketing.com/speaker-bonus (goodies folks get from my live seminar)

doitmarketing.com/speak (all the companion tools and downloads for THIS book!)

 **39** **SPEAKER WEBSITE RULE #4**

Rule number 4 for your website is to **automate your follow-up** to generate top-of-mind awareness. And this can be simple: an email newsletter that goes out once or twice a month, an auto responder series, blogs, the occasional special offer, subscriber-only content that you share with your list as your list starts to grow—whatever it is, you want to keep that cycle going.

So many speakers build a list—actually so many speakers *don't* build the list—but if they do build a list, they never email those subscribers. (Guilty as charged—I did this back in the first two or three years of my own speaking business. Fun fact: I used Yahoo Groups for my rare "once-every-whenever-I-remembered-to-do-it" email blasts if you can imagine back to the stone ages of the internet!)

Let's say that they opted into your list or they were in your audience a year ago, two years ago, three years ago, and you decide to email them. Suddenly, one day out of the blue, they get this random email, and now it looks like spam because they totally forgot who you are. They forgot where they met you. They forgot that association meeting three years ago.

There's an old saying, "The best time to plant a tree is twenty years ago, the second best time to plant a tree is today"—so start your list-building and automated follow-up sequence today!

40 SPEAKER WEBSITE RULE #5

Next rule: ***Show* people—don't tell—why they should hire you.** One of the assignments from a previous chapter was to create your buying criteria: twenty questions to ask before hiring any motivational speaker; twenty questions to ask before hiring any marketing speaker; ten reasons to hire you; seven reasons why you're going to rock their next meeting, etc.

Now **put that document on your website** or a landing page so your clients can see it or so that you can email that link to an interested client any time you want to.

Example: www.BestMarketingCoach.com. See how that works?

41 SPEAKER WEBSITE RULE #6

You want to have printable PDFs of all your one-sheets, program descriptions, and key documents—simply formatted, bold, clean design—so prospects can download hard copies easily.

It's important to not just have your program descriptions on your web pages.

Here's why nicely formatted PDFs are important: Decisionmakers sometimes don't make decisions in a vacuum. They walk you into a meeting, meaning they're going to forward that PDF or they're going to print off copies of that PDF and give copies to everyone around the table.

Buyers still want to print things out. Don't ask me why, it's just the truth. They print it off so they can throw it in their briefcase and look at it on the plane; whatever their reason: **Buyers use printers!**

Ever tried printing a web page? Broken graphics, funky margins, weird lines, odd text breaks, you've seen it. Disaster. **Easily printed PDF downloads that look great are a must.**

42 SPEAKER WEBSITE RULE #7

Build credibility with your "About" page.

Another hugely important section of your website is your "About" page. Your "About" page or speaker bio is where you get to pull out all your indisputable points of proof. Who you are, where you came from, what you've done.

I remember the day this was made clear to me. I was talking to a meeting planner and we were early in the prospect conversation, and the prospect says, "So, David, what have you done?"

Meaningful pause.

I said, "Well, I'm not sure what you mean. What do you mean what have I done?"

And she says, "Well, I went to your website and I'm downloading all your stuff and I see speaker and author and all your programs and your client list. But *before you became a speaker*, what did you do?"

 **@dnewman**

Meeting planners want to know: What value did you bring to the world before you became a speaker?

I was floored. I never even thought that would be a question.

But you know what . . . it's *everybody's* question.

On that day in 2006, I might as well have told that meeting planner, "Let me get back to you in about three days with a good answer to that." Which was not a good answer, by the way!

What really happened? I was fumbling and bumbling and hemming and hawing. Bad!

When you tell your story, don't just talk about what you're selling today.

Tell the whole story. **How did you come to do what you do? Why do you do what you do and whom you do it for?**

 # 43 SPEAKER WEBSITE RULE #8

Don't include pricing on your website.

I get this question a lot. Should I put my pricing on the website? Should I have my fees up there?

The answer is yes, no, and maybe.

It can really go one of two ways, and it's up to you to see what fits best for you.

Philosophy number 1 is: Do NOT include pricing.

The reason is that you are going to regret losing business on the low end AND the high end if you put a number out there and that's regardless of what the number is.

Philosophy number 2 is: DO put pricing up because it becomes objective reality.

Folks who are looking to invest and are serious will contact you.

And the broke-ass losers won't.

In the end, it's a judgment call based on your preference or your career status, where you are in your speaking career: early, mid-career, or more seasoned.

If you're wishy-washy on your fees, then don't publish them.

If you're rock solid, then do.

For example, when clients want me to come and speak, it's $15,000 to $20,000 all day, every day, any place and any time so I have zero fear about putting that number out there. I don't put pants on for less than $15,000. So why should I be coy and play games?

It could also be a matter of your existing speaker bureau relationships. If you have bureaus that say your fee is $10,000 and your website says $5,500, that's going to be a problem. If the speaker bureaus say your fee is $5,500 and your website says $10,000, that's also going to be a problem. Depending on how and where and who's reselling you and who's referencing your fees, you want to make sure to always stay in alignment.

44 DON'T BE AN IDIOT ABOUT YOUR FEES

Before you go to the marketplace, you have to be

rock solid on your fees.

I remember working with a fairly successful speaker. She had her CSP (Certified Speaking Professional) designation from the National Speakers Association. Like all of us, she had good times and bad times, highs and lows.

She said to me, "David, I am all over the map. I've charged $1,500 and I've charged $15,000. I just don't know what my fee is anymore. You tell me."

She had gotten gigs for $15,000 and she'd taken gigs for $1,500 and she didn't know who she was anymore.

She was playing speaker-fee roulette: "What's today's fee? I don't know."

How scary and sad is that?

 @dnewman
You MUST have a clear and tangible idea of your market value as a speaker.

If you've done the competitive scan we talked about earlier in the book, you've identified your leading competitors. If you are competing with other speakers or other consultants, maybe their fees aren't quite as visible, but any consultant, any trainer that does any amount of speaking (and does it successfully), will probably have one or more speaker bureau relationships. This means you can put in their name and "speaker fee" into Google and find their fees or fee ranges.

Here's another tip: **Don't be an egomaniac.** For the speaker I mentioned above, $1,500 was absolutely too low. But $15,000 was absolutely too high. Her market value was somewhere in between. It was way more than $1,500 but it sure as heck wasn't $15,000. The problem is that she had trained herself to take whatever fee she could negotiate and that's it.

@dnewman

Don't be an egomaniac—be real. Remember, it's not the fee you charge, it's the fee you get.

When I ask my speaker clients what fee they are charging, they'll throw out a number like, "Oh, I charge $12,000." My second question is, "Have you ever gotten that fee?" Then the phone gets eerily quiet before they say, "I got that fee once. For a three-day program." Dude, $12,000 for a three-day program is $4,000 a day. That is dramatically different from a $12,000 speaking fee.

Get serious. Get real. And you'll get much better at making a living.

45 AVOID TAXI-METER PRICING

I had a client who was a speaker in the financial services industry. Prior to speaking, she was a stockbroker and highly successful investment advisor herself; she'd written a book and was speaking around the country. When she came to me, her fee schedule was the following:

* 30 minutes, $7,500
* 45 minutes, $9,000
* 1 hour, $10,500
* 75 minutes, $12,000

Do you see what's going on there?

She was literally charging her speaking clients in fifteen-minute increments!

That doesn't make any sense at all because it's what I call "**taxi-meter pricing**." They are not buying you by the minute or the mile or the word or the pound. You're not a stick of salami!

If you want to have more than one fee, there are only three fees you should ever quote:

- ✳ Up to half day (including keynote)
- ✳ Full day
- ✳ Multi-day

That is it. Simple for you to remember—simple to share with clients— simple for them to understand.

The other option is just a single number ($4,500 or $7,500 or $15,000, whatever your fee is) per day. Whether you are onstage for twenty minutes or seven hours, it's the same fee.

Imagine the simplicity of this sales conversation if your speaking fee is $7,500 . . .

Can you give a ten-minute keynote? Sure. *How much is that?* $7,500.

Can you be with us all day and do a one-hour keynote then a two-hour workshop, moderate the panel at lunch, emcee the awards in the afternoon, and kick off our Hall of Fame dinner? Yes. *How much is that?* $7,500.

Now when you offer this to meeting planners, conference producers, and association executives, every single one of them is going to be VERY pleasantly surprised.

I remember one client for whom we tailored a deal like this. She audibly gasped and said, "All the other speakers I'm talking to were charging extra for all those things. I was feeling nickel and dimed—a thousand extra for that, two thousand extra for this. You're willing to do EVERYTHING for one fee?"

My response? "Yes, and that's why I'm your next keynote speaker. Let's do this."

After all, once you're in Kansas City to keynote this event, you're not going to be in Orlando at lunch and you're not going to be in San Diego at night. You're there all day until your plane goes wheels up at the airport. So why not serve the daylights out of that client for the fee they'll gladly invest with you to get all that value?

Why do I recommend you do this? Because the longer that client and those audience members are exposed to you, the better for you and for your marketing, the more spin-off, the more repeat and referral business you're going to get.

When you're there for the full day, you become like family. I become like Uncle David. And I just love extended multiple contacts with an audience. I'm teaching. I'm catalyzing. I'm building rapport, connection, and relationship as the "friendly expert," and at the end of the day, they're far more likely to feel like they've gotten to know you, like you, and trust you.

You can be in a room full of several hundred people, and at the end of the day, you're at your book signing or the cocktail party, and an audience member will tell you, "*You know, it felt like you were talking to me one-on-one.*" That's because they saw you in two or three or four different contexts. They saw you deliver content. They saw you facilitate. They saw you moderate. They heard your funny crazy stories. They saw you let your guard down and become one of them.

You have to decide whether this works for you or not.

Does it make sense to have an all-you-can-eat speaking fee? For me it's a huge benefit because you know what? I'm going to be cooling my heels at the airport anyway. If I'm speaking from 9:00 a.m. to 10:30 a.m., here's what the rest of my day looks like: Ten thirty to eleven thirty, sign books, shake hands, kiss babies, then head out. Twelve o'clock, grab a hamburger at the McDonald's at the airport, cool my heels for two hours, wait at my gate. Two thirty, the flight leaves. Five thirty, I'm back in Philadelphia.

So why not take the nine o'clock flight, do the whole day, and make three hundred new friends? Get spin-off business. Repeat business. Referral business. Build relationships, get introductions, and make personal connections with so many more people in that audience. And let's not forget about the tremendous value you'd deliver to that meeting planner.

Does it make economic sense for you to have keynote, half-day, and full-day fees, or are you better off saying, "You know what? I'm there anyway—it's one fee. Pay one price. No guessing. Use me as much as you possibly can"?

> 🐦 **@dnewman**
> Offer one speaking fee for an entire day (and encourage clients to USE you 100 percent) .

To download your Speaking Fee Profit Maximizer, visit doitmarketing .com/speak.

46 DON'T CHARGE LIKE AN AMATEUR

 @dnewman

There MUST be a floor to your fee. It's the "professional speaker minimum wage." Charge less and you'll lose business.

Putting my conference producer hat onto my head, back when I was hiring speakers, there was a base "minimum credibility" number for speaking fees.

There still is. And what's interesting is that this base minimum credibility number probably hasn't changed for 10+ years in spite of inflation, deflation, or flatulation.

 @dnewman

The base minimum credible speaking fee is $4,500. If your fee is LESS than $4,500, you are positioning yourself as an amateur.

Did I just pull this number out of a hat?

No, I did not.

Here's where I got that number. I was having a conversation with a meeting planner, and although I ended up not being the best fit for her event, I said to her, "Now that it's over, do you mind giving me five minutes of your brainpower?"

Oh yeah sure, David, go ahead. (This is how I get more actionable market intelligence from my nos than you probably get from your yeses!)

I asked, "What fee range do you find yourself hiring most of your speakers?"

Without hesitation, she said, "Most of the speakers we hire are between $5,000 and $10,000."

She continued, "We've hired speakers for less than $5,000 and we found that they just weren't that good. We've also hired speakers for $15,000 to $25,000 and a lot of them were disappointing too. The best speakers we found consistently are in that $5,000 to $10,000 range."

This particular question and conversation has played out dozens of times over the years and the answers are invariably the same.

Hold that data point in your mind and rewind the clock to about 2005, when I was still doing corporate training. I had a training contract with QVC, so if you like shopping, if you've ever bought anything from QVC, thank you, some of that money went in to my pocket.

I sat down with the head of training at QVC and I asked her the same question. What was the typical fee range for the outside trainers, facilitators, and consultants that she hired? And without missing a beat, she said, "*The most we're used to paying an outside speaker is $4,500.*"

The reason is that QVC was buying a commodity. They were looking for ANY time management trainer, for ANY leadership coach, nothing special, just routine day training for which they didn't pay more than $4,500.

Fun fact: As of this writing, according to https://www.usinflationcalculator.com, the value of $4,500 in 2005 is $5,816.57 today.

Meanwhile, the meeting planners have consistently told me over the past ten years that they were most comfortable hiring speakers in the $5,000 to $10,000 fee range.

> 🐦 **@dnewman**
>
> If your speaking fee is at least $4,500, you are at the crossroads of credible and affordable.

You're at the high end of QVC (not even adjusting for inflation—*you're a bargain*!), and the low end of what other decisionmakers need to pay to take you seriously.

You are straddling the proverbial speaking fee sweet spot!

Now your fees are going to depend on where you are in your career, on your credibility and your visibility and your "fame," because we're all famous in some little niche, some little area where we are rock stars. If you're the big fish in that small pond and you've got a strong reputation, maybe you've got some books, you've got a great website, you have awesome programs, you have a fancy client list, go higher: $7,500, $9,500, $12,000, $15,000, $20,000. These are the common speaking-fee levels for the typical clients we work with.

But please remember: *Never any less than $4,500* because you will undermine the perception of your expertise.

 @dnewman

Never worry about "pricing yourself out of the market." Worry about how much you need to raise your speaking fee to price yourself INTO the market where premium clients are looking to hire premium speakers at premium fees.

 # 47 DON'T START TOO LOW OR GO TOO SLOW

There are so many speakers I know where, early in their careers, they started quoting speaking fees that were **too low**. And it's been stagnating there for years.

An even worse problem is seasoned speakers who go **too slow** in elevating and escalating their fees over time as their careers evolve.

One highly successful speaker I worked with came to me with a fee of $10,000. He quoted that and got it regularly with very little fee resistance.

He knew where to prospect, what to say, and how to sell. He closed $10K speaking gigs all day long. No problem there.

I asked him, "How many years has your fee been at $10,000?" And then the phone goes a little bit quiet there for two seconds and he says, *Gosh, it's been $10,000 for the last ten years.*

He had been getting $10,000 per speech for the last ten years.

I told him, "I have good news and I have bad news. Seven years ago, you should've raised your fee to $12,500. Four years ago, you should've raised your fee to $15,000, and right about now you could be raising your fee to $17,500. But don't worry. Let's do an experiment. The next time the phone rings, I want you to quote $12,500." He agrees to humor me in our little experiment.

A week later he calls me up and says, "Dude, you just put $5,000 in my pocket." (I always love when clients say things like that.)

I asked him what he meant. He said a client called his office and they wanted him to present for two days and asked for his fee.

He quoted them $12,500 per day, and the client said, "That works— that's 25K for our event, right?" Right. At his old fee, he would've quoted $20K, and at his new fee, he got $25K.

The lesson? Start at the right fee and then get to know when to ratchet it up.

My rule of thumb is that if you've been getting the same fee for eighteen months to two years consistently, it's time to raise the fee. Every eighteen to twenty-four months, your fee goes up.

Let's say your speaking fee is $3,500 today. First of all, you're not $3,500 anymore, because right now, when you put this book down, you're at $4,500, right? Remember the "professional speaker minimum wage"!

After you've been getting $4,500 for eighteen to twenty-four months, now you're at $5,500. Go to the market with that, and in another eighteen to twenty-four months, now you're at $6,500. You do that for another couple years, now you're at $7,500.

 @dnewman

Your speaking fee can go up as fast or slow as you want, but you do NOT want fee stagnation because that means you're leaving free money on the table.

48 AVOID THE "WRONG WORK" PRICING TRAP

Here's another crazy thing that sometimes hap-pens with your speaking fee.

You have to think like a buyer. If you're not getting booked with fees that you want for the work that you want, there's something screwy with your fee schedule.

For example, I worked with a speaker a few years ago who said, "David, I'm getting an awful lot of training gigs. I'm hardly getting any keynotes."

I asked, "How much do you charge for a training program?" His answer was $3,500.

"How much do you charge for a keynote?" His answer was $7,500.

Now if you're the buyer, which one would you hire him for?

Of course, you're going to buy a lot more training from this guy. No one's hiring him for keynotes and most clients hire him for training because the economic incentive on this fee schedule was upside down and backward to his goals.

If you want to do a lot more keynotes and a lot less training, your keynote fee should be cheaper than your training. Watch how soon you'll start to sell more keynotes.

Treat pricing as an incentive and a guide so that you can do the kind of work that you want to do at a good fee and so that you don't have to do the kind of work that you hate.

Look at your fee schedule. Are you offering a better deal on the work you hate? Flip your prices.

Do you not feel like schlepping around the world, spending half your life on overnight flights? Demand prohibitive fees for that (and cross your fingers that no one comes up with your prohibitive fee!).

I once got invited to speak in Iran for $3,500. I don't speak in Philadelphia for $3,500, let alone go to Iran for $3,500. That's one where I quoted my international fees starting at $25,000, because I simply did not want to go.

49 SEVENTEEN GREAT ANSWERS TO "HOW MUCH DO YOU CHARGE?"

 @dnewman

For professional speakers and thought-leading executives and entrepreneurs . . . the #1 dreaded question is, "How much do you charge?"

Especially when it's asked **too early**, **out of context**, and **before you've established** any sort of **relationship** with the prospect or any sort of **value** for the project . . .

In short, if you blow the answer, your prospect is gone.

Here are three things **NOT** to do:

1. Quote a random price out of thin air (unless you sell haircuts for $18 or oil changes for $34.95 or you do bookkeeping for $65/hr).
2. Act surprised or unprepared for the question ("Uhhh . . . what do you mean?").
3. Get defensive or go on a rant about how "all people care about these days is price, price, price."

Some of the answers you're about to get are **evergreen**, some **you can adapt to your own personality**, and some you may want to **keep in reserve until just the right moment** with just the right prospect.

Here we go . . .

"How Much Do You Charge?"

1. A lot. Why do you ask?
2. I don't think we're there yet because I don't know what you're buying.
3. I'll answer your question in a moment, but to give you a more accurate answer, may I ask you three questions first?
4. Well, the friends and family rate might apply but we're not friends yet—do you mind if I ask you a few friendly questions that will help us answer your pricing question together?
5. It's nine million dollars until I know what you're buying. Can we spend a few minutes narrowing that down to help you lower the price?
6. I have good news and I have bad news. The good news is that you don't have a $500,000 problem. The bad news is that you don't have a $10,000 problem, either . . . if you can help me answer some key questions, we'll both know a lot more about what your investment might look like.
7. If it works, it's cheap. If it doesn't, it's expensive.
8. Let's talk about what you're trying to accomplish first and then we'll work out some pricing options based on that.
9. Do you want the Ferrari version, the Lexus version, or the VW Bug?
10. A project like the one you're asking about ranges from $X to $Y. Sometimes a little more. Not usually less. Is that what you were expecting to invest?
11. There's no good answer to that question in a vacuum. Can we talk a little more about what you're hoping we can do for you? Then I'll give you some pricing options that make sense for your budget.
12. A project of this scope only makes sense if it's already in your budget. Nobody wakes up one day and suddenly finds the money to solve these kinds of problems. If you can share the budget range you have set aside for this, I can tell you if it makes sense for us to talk any further.

13. I have a feeling that if I quote a random number right now, I'll be dead in the water. Do you mind if I ask you some questions to get a better idea of what your goals are? Then the numbers we talk about will be specific to you and your situation.

14. Just like you need to make an educated decision about which partner or resource to hire, I need to give you an educated answer to your pricing question. And I'm feeling pretty dumb right now, since we just started talking. Mind if we have a ten-minute conversation about your situation? After that, I'll have a much better idea of what you're after and some different ways we can help.

15. Sounds like price is the most important factor to you. In my experience, everything is expensive until you want it. Can we talk about what you want and then work our way to the pricing options based on that?

16. It's more than a cab ride to [local landmark, e.g., "the Empire State Building"] but less than [the landmark, e.g., "the building"]. If we can chat for ten minutes about why you called, I can give you a much more specific answer. Do you have ten minutes now or shall we look at our calendars?

17. Until I have a better idea of what you want—and whether or not we can even help—any number I give you is going to be too high. Would it be OK if we spend a few minutes discussing why you called? Then if we can help, I'll get you the pricing options you need. And if we can't, I'll refer you to some other great resources that do things we don't. Fair enough?

50 SALT AND PEPPER YOUR FEE

Some people are uncomfortable charging a serious, credible speaking fee.

For that reason, they immediately start giving prospects a way out by quoting their number and immediately adding on phrases like, "I can work with your budget," "I'm flexible," and "unless that's too high." I wish I were kidding.

Here's an exercise to overcome your discomfort with $4,500 or $5,500 or whatever your new fee is.

This is my famous "Salt-Pepper-My-Fee exercise" and it has helped many of my newer speaking clients get comfortable with quoting that minimum-wage fee of $4,500.

Sit down at your kitchen table and take out your saltshaker, a pepper mill, and a Post-it Note upon which you'll write down your speaking fee: $4,500 for the purpose of this exercise.

For the next ten minutes, take your index finger and point to the salt and say, "That's salt."

And then point to the pepper and say, "That's pepper."

Point to the Post-it Note and say, "And my fee is $4,500."

And now just pointing at these three items in random order over and over while saying out loud:

- ✳ "There's salt, that's pepper, my fee is $4,500."
- ✳ "My fee is $4,500, and that's the pepper and there's the salt."
- ✳ "Pepper, my fee is $4,500, and that's the salt."

It is a statement of fact.

It's right in front of you.

Obvious. Clear. No waffling or hemming or hawing, right?

Do you say, "Maybe it's salt, but I can be flexible"? No, it's salt. What's the black stuff? The black stuff is pepper. Do you say, "Maybe it's pepper one day and paprika on a different day"? No. It's pepper. It always has been pepper. It always will be pepper. Stone-cold fact, that's pepper.

What's your fee? $4,500. It is what it is. How much does it cost to have you come in and speak to my group? $4,500. My speaking fee? Oh, that's $4,500. How much is it? For the type of program we just discussed, I get $4,500.

Spend ten minutes doing this exercise. Out loud. Yes. Really!!

This is salt and my fee is $4,500. This is pepper.
Pepper, salt, $4,500.
Salt, pepper, $4,500.
Salt, $4,500, pepper.
$4,500, pepper, salt
Point, point, point. It's as clear as the nose on your face.

And the next time you present your fee to a real live prospect (which is NOT when they first ask, but we'll get to that later in this book), your fee is your fee—and it's no longer an embarrassing catastrophe for you to quote the number you deserve calmly, casually, organically, and comfortably.

Not maybe, not sometimes, not "but we can negotiate," not "if you have the budget." Your fee is the fee whether they have the budget or not.

The fee is the fee is the fee.

DO IT! SUCCESS STRATEGY:
HOW TO MARKET YOUR ONLINE COURSE SO THE RIGHT PEOPLE BUY

BY DAVID SITEMAN GARLAND

I remember many years ago when I was attending an event, someone was complaining about her customers.

Errrr . . . complaining is an understatement. RANTING.

She was talking about how her customers were not putting in the work to get results from her online course.

They were, in fact, complaining about doing work.

At every small obstacle . . . they gave up.

And she was VERY frustrated.

I remember someone looking at her dead in the eye and saying, "Well, they are YOUR customers. That's your fault for not attracting and marketing to the right people."

Ouch.

The blood seemed to literally escape her face.

I mean she turned WHITE.

Then, I saw the anger starting to set in.

Finally, she said, "It's not my fault . . . it's their fault! My course is great. They are just lazy."

She then walked away (I almost feel like she stuck her tongue out before she walked away . . . but I might be remembering that wrong).

But, here is the thing. That straight shooter who looked her dead in the eye is 100 percent right.

Who you market to and who you attract is UP TO YOU.

And how you go about this makes a huge difference between getting the right vs. wrong customers (and yes . . . there is a major difference).

Because you want customers who will DO THE WORK.

(continues)

SALT AND PEPPER YOUR FEE

121

We are in the results business. You want customers who come in, put their hard hat on, follow your course/program, and get themselves some good old-fashioned killer results (with your guidance along the way).

What are some tips?

1. Avoid unrealistic timelines in your marketing. Timelines can often be awesome . . . if they are realistic. But, losing fifty pounds in ten days? Um, I don't think so. That will attract people looking for a quick fix. Losing a pound a week for the next three months? Much more realistic. Those will attract two different types of customers. Words matter.

2. Avoid the overhyped promise. You'll make $7 zillion with an ebook! Every successful course has a result associated with it . . . that's a good (and necessary) thing. But, it has to be realistic and tangible. A better (more realistic) result would be that if you do everything in the course as instructed, you will complete your ebook and launch it. For example, in my List-A-Palooza course that is inside of my Create Awesome Online Courses program, we teach people that don't have an email list how to build one from scratch to five hundred to one thousand people (and people who already have a list to add an additional five hundred to one thousand). Notice . . . five hundred to one thousand. Not one hundred thousand. Realistic expectations = realistic results (and happy customers).

3. DO talk about work. This is huge. Your course takes work for your customers to complete it and get results. You are giving people the exact blueprint, but they have to put in the work and effort to get that baby done. And it's probably a lot of work! However, of course, your course is the shortcut that saves them tons of time and money if they were trying to do it on their own. Don't shy away in your marketing from mentioning the work and perseverance needed. Otherwise, you are going to attract people looking for the "latest flavor of the month" or something where "any more effort than pushing a button is too much effort" or even worse . . . the "one thing goes wrong and I'm giving up!" peeps. Yuck. You don't want that. Ain't nobody got time for those peeps.

Bottom line is who you market to and attract is in YOUR control. Choose your words and strategies wisely and talk directly to those perfect-fit clients. Good things will happen.

David Siteman Garland *is the creator of The Rise to the Top and Create Awesome Online Courses. David helps people create and sell online courses, with over five thousand students in over a hundred countries who have created successful courses on everything from kindergarten teaching to snowboarding. To get started and learn how you can create, promote, and profit from your own online course, sign up for his 100 percent free training at CreateAwesomeOnlineCourses.com.*

 **51 THE FIRST NUMBER SHOULD NEVER BE YOUR FEE**

Here's a sales "A-ha!" moment: Numbers scare the

hell out of your prospects.

Specifically—YOUR numbers scare them. Even on the phone, you can almost feel a prospect clench their teeth and tense up when it comes to discussing pricing.

Good news: Although your numbers are scary, their own numbers don't scare them at all.

Putting those two concepts together, if your numbers scare your prospects but their own numbers don't scare them at all . . .

For example, if you're having a very nice prospect conversation and you're talking about their event and their goals and their company and their team and their initiatives, all of a sudden out of the blue pops up the question, "By the way, this all sounds great. How much would it cost to bring you in?"

Now, if you drop your number on them and say, "Well, my speaking fee is $9,500," they're going to go into sticker shock. Their heads are going to blow up. Why? Because they have no context for that number.

ANY number with no context is going to sound incredibly expensive. You're going to lose deal after deal after deal. And by the way, I don't care if your number is $9,500, $4,500, or $15,000. A number without a framework is a number that's too high.

Let's build that framework so that your fee is NEVER the first number that comes up in your sales conversations.

52 CONTEXT OF VALUE AND CONTRAST OF SCALE

Let's say you're talking about doing a leadership training program for a company who wants to train twenty of their mid-level executives. You're talking to the person responsible for this group.

Here are some questions you might ask to introduce THEIR numbers into your sales conversation long before your fee structure ever comes up:

YOU: *So, Bob, to give me a good flavor of the group, to give me an idea of their level, what's the average salary of these managers and leaders that you're putting into the group? Is it about $50,000?*

PROSPECT: *Oh, no, these guys are a little bit more senior. These guys are about $80,000 average salary.*

YOU: *And, Bob, you said there's about twenty of them.*

PROSPECT: *Yes.*

YOU: *Okay, great. So we're looking at impacting about $1.6 million of payroll. This talent pool that's going to be in this workshop represents about $1.6 million of payroll value. Am I doing the math right?*

PROSPECT: *Yeah, that's about right.*

What's the magic of this particular piece of the sales conversation? You are using THEIR numbers: twenty executives, $80,000 salary. You're doing the math. That's twenty times $80,000 equals $1.6 million. Then you're confirming your math with your prospect and gaining their explicit agreement to your calculations.

You can do this lots of ways: Ask about average salary of employees, cost of turnover, average deal size, average sale, customer lifetime value, and so on. If you're selling a health and wellness program, ask about benefits cost containment. If you're selling a corporate culture program, ask about recruiting and retention costs. If you're selling a time management seminar, ask about the hard value of their employees' time plus the opportunity cost of what they're not making time for. You get the idea.

Here's another example:

YOU: *You sell these big industrial HVAC units that sit on top of hotels and corporate office buildings. What does one of these things cost? Is this a $20,000 item? Is it a $200,000 item?*

PROSPECT: *Our big HVAC generators that sit on top of buildings are $120,000 each.*

YOU: *And so if a Marriott or Hilton buys one of these for a property, about how many do they buy?*

PROSPECT: *Oh, they usually need to buy three.*

YOU: *So your average deal size, am I doing the math right, is about $360,000?*

PROSPECT: *Yes.*

YOU: *And about how many deals do each of these salespeople do in a given year?*

PROSPECT: *Well, they're incentivized to do between ten and twelve.*

YOU: *Really? That's 3.6 million dollars' worth of HVAC units.*

PROSPECT: *You got it.*

YOU: *Great. And how many salespeople do you want to put through our program?*

PROSPECT: *Ten.*

YOU: *So we can potentially impact $36 million of new sales revenue. Is that right?*

PROSPECT: *I never thought about it like that, but yes that's about right.*

To download your "Speaker Dollarization Worksheet," visit doitmarketing .com/speak.

This is important because you can't possibly serve them as a speaker, as a trainer, as a coach, as a consultant, as an outside expert unless you know what's at stake—and what kind of impact can you make—in terms of dollars and cents.

If you're not asking these key questions about value, impact, results, and outcomes, you're just flying blind and then your fee has no context of value or contrast of scale.

Start asking financial and business questions and they'll start giving you financial and business answers.

Here's a great overarching question: What are they trying to accomplish?

No one brings in a speaker because they have a speaker problem.

No one brings in a trainer because they have a training problem.

They bring in speakers, trainers, and consultants because they have **business** problems.

And those business problems have a hard economic value and you need to dig and bring to the surface those economic impact indicators; find out what they're trying to accomplish and find out what needles they're trying to move, what results are they trying to get, what outcome are they trying to achieve?

If you do anything less in your discovery conversations, then you are guilty of sales malpractice because now you're selling widgets instead of solving problems.

53 WHAT DOES 1 PERCENT LOOK LIKE?

So now you've got some of their numbers on the
table. We talked about the twenty executives, $80,000 average salary, 20 x $80k is $1.6 million of payroll value.

Now you're positioned to ask, "What would a 1 percent improvement look like? What would a 2 percent improvement look like? What if we move the needle 5 percent on this result? What if we move the needle 10 percent on this result?"

For example, if you're impacting $1.6 million dollars of payroll and you make those twenty leaders 10 percent more effective at doing their jobs, boosting their efficiency, their productivity, and their results—in other words, you make them 10 percent better leaders, 10 percent of $1.6 million dollars is $160,000. I have good news: My speaking fee is a lot less than $160,000 and I bet yours is less than that too!

Even a 5 percent improvement comes to $80,000 of value that drops right to their bottom line. And a mere 2.5 percent improvement gets them $40,000 of return. If your speaking or training fee is $7,500 and you just showed them you'll deliver $40,000 of value in exchange for a $7,500 investment, that's the best deal they've seen in a long time.

Do you see how that's dramatically different than, "Hey, what's your speaking fee?" and you reply, "My fee is $7,500"?

When we talk prospects through their math, their value, their ROI, it becomes a completely different ball game.

And it's a game that you'll win more often than not.

 # 54 "CAN YOU PUT A NUMBER ON IT?"

 **@dnewman**

Here's a key sales question you need to ask persistently: "Can you put a number on it?"

When a prospect says things like, "Our production times are slow," you come back with, "Can you put a number on it?"

We're falling behind in sales. *Can you put a number on it?*

Turnover is getting too high. *Can you put a number on it?*

Morale is slipping. *Can you put a number on it?*

Hours, dollars, percentages, profits, sales, margin, cost, whatever the metrics are, can you put a number on it?

Can you put a number on it? Can you put a number on it? Can you put a number on it?

That needs to become your mantra in every sales conversation.

Here's the secret: If they **can't** put a number on it, then they're probably not the economic decisionmaker.

Because if you find who owns the problem that you solve, believe me, they know in a heartbeat what the numbers are, what the impact is, what the financial and business implications are of having the problem and of solving the problem.

If you're getting a whole lot of "I don't know. I have no idea. I don't know where to begin even answering that question," then you know you're talking to a gatekeeper or a lackey or a subordinate and you're not talking to the real economic decisionmaker.

DO IT! SUCCESS STRATEGY: BYPASS THE GATEKEEPERS TO SELL TO TRADE ASSOCIATIONS AND PROFESSIONAL SOCIETIES

BY ED RIGSBEE, CSP, CAE

Instantly boost your association bookings by getting smart. Stop calling the meeting planners.

First, meeting planners receive an endless stream of speaker and speaker bureau sales phone calls. Getting through is nearly impossible.

(continues)

Second, more times than not, the meeting planner is simply the logistics person and not the decisionmaker. In order to sell yourself, you must access the decisionmaker. While sometimes it might be the meeting planner, more times it is the executive director, chief operating officer, or the director of meetings and events . . . or possibly, a volunteer committee leader. And there is one more important element: People do not always tell the truth and admit they are not the decisionmaker. You don't realize it, but you are spending your precious time barking up the wrong tree.

The association gatekeepers, as you already know, do a great job of keeping speakers out. With this in mind, how does one determine who the decisionmaker really is?

Make your life easy and go around the brick wall straight to the more accurate information.

Call the association/society publication editor. They are not inundated with phone calls. They have no ego-driven reason to keep the truth from you as to who the speaker buyer decisionmaker really is. If you make a reasonable "relationship bank" deposit with the editor, there is a good chance you can make an immediate withdrawal—ask who the true decisionmaker is on the events side of the organization.

It works like this:

Write articles based on your expertise and/or book(s). Be sure they are quality work at the level that editors will publish them. You'll want to have a minimum of six and have the articles uploaded to your website—each article should be a separate webpage. At the Rigsbee.com "Article Bank," you'll find over two hundred articles within eight sub-categories. Don't be intimidated as I've been at this for thirty years. However, use my website as a guide. Change your website navigation tab from "Blog" to "Article Bank," to make it look like you are a player. Most magazine pages are about 700 words so that is a great word count to start. A range of articles having word counts from 600 to 1,500 words is even better.

Skip the gatekeeper and call the association publications editor and give your articles to the association publication. Generally, you can find their name at the association/society's website in the "About Us" section. Sometimes their title is director of communications. Be generous; make plenty of relationship bank deposits, as it will pay off quickly. At this step, building a relationship with the editor is crucial to your success. Be sure to ask a lot of questions about the needs of their members and then recommend which of your articles might be right for them.

After your conversation with the editor, use the "Columbo Close" to leverage the relationship by asking, just before you hang up: "Before I let you go, would you please tell me who it is that decides on speakers for the organization's events?" They will say something like, "Our meeting planner is Suzie." You thank them and ask, "Does Suzie actually make the buying decisions on speakers?" If they say yes, bridge relationship to Suzie by asking to be connected. If they say no, actually Jane makes the decisions, she is our executive director, say thanks and ask to be connected. An internal transfer gets through far more frequently than an outside call.

When you connect with the decisionmaker . . . whether the executive director or a volunteer leader meeting committee chair . . . mention that you had just made a number of your articles available to the organization's publication, ask about the challenges of the members . . . similar to the discussion with the editor. Then say something like, "Would you please tell me about your speaker selection process?" Sometimes they are currently selecting, selected last week, or will be doing so in X number of months down the road. This is the point where effective traditional selling starts. Follow-up will determine your success. If you are lucky enough to talk about their speaker needs today, that's awesome. Sell, sell, sell—however, more times than not you will need to get back at a very specific time. Put it into your CRM and follow up when appropriate. It generally takes

(continues)

five to ten callbacks to seal the deal. One more thing: Ask about their other meetings such as:

* Board meetings
* Sales, marketing, or leadership summits
* Regional meetings
* Association executive council meetings (state chapter executive directors)
* Etc.

Remember, many membership organizations have more than just their annual convention where they need speakers. And the decisionmaker for the other meetings might be a different person, so be sure to ask.

In the United States alone, there are over 100,000 national, regional, state, and local associations and societies. There is plenty of business for you and everyone else. The key to instant success is to use your articles as the relationship-building conduit in order to find the true decisionmaker. From that point, it is all about bulldog selling . . . keeping at it. Stay in contact until they say "yes" or "no." If they say "no," it is okay . . . start to think about how you can get on their program the following year and put your plan into action.

Ed Rigsbee, CSP, CAE, has his feet firmly planted on both sides of the membership organization fence. He has been teaching professional speakers and consultants his proprietary "go to market" system for over twenty years. In addition to serving as CEO of an IRS-recognized 501(c)3 public charity, he is the author of the seminal membership organization growth guide The ROI of Membership—Today's Missing Link for Explosive Growth. If you would like to attend one of his amazing Selling to Associations Intensive workshops hosted in Las Vegas, visit SellingToAssociations.com.

55 "YOUR FEE IS TOO HIGH" IS ALWAYS A LIE

You've heard it. *Your fee is too high!* This kills a lot of speakers because it's both a trap and a lie.

It's a **trap** because when a prospect tells most speakers that their fee is too high, they'll say, "*Yeah, I know, I'll lower it for you. You're right. I shouldn't charge $7,500. How about $3,500? How about $1,200? How about no fee and just a nice suite in the hotel?*"

 @dnewman

"Your fee is too high" means that you blew the sales conversation.

And let me tell you three problems that it's not:

Number 1, it's not about your **fee**.

Number 2, it's not about your **program**.

And number 3, it's not even about their **budget**.

"Your fee is too high" is a **lie** because what they really mean is that they don't believe you can solve their problem.

It is 100 percent about their confidence level in your ability to deliver value and results in terms of their problems, heartaches, headaches, challenges, goals, achievements, initiatives, strategies, what they're trying to accomplish.

Simply put: They don't believe you.

It's a confidence problem and it's about their confidence in your solution.

And what this also means is that you either didn't use their numbers to frame the context of value and show the contrast of scale or you tried to sell a speech. You didn't try to help them solve a big problem or get them a meaningful outcome that's truly important to them.

As a buyer, if I'm buying a speech, $50 is too high.

As a buyer, if I'm buying a solution to a problem—and I may have a $500,000 problem—I'd be eager to spend $50,000 for your year-long consulting package to solve my $500,000 problem.

Fifty dollars for a speaker that has zero value? That's $50 too much. Fifty thousand dollars to solve a $500,000 problem? That's the bargain of the year. You, my friend, need to become the bargain of the year!

 # 56 USE BRIDGING LANGUAGE TO SEAL THE DEAL

One of the smartest ways to gain buyer commit- ment is to ask prospects about goals and metrics. Ask them about where they are and ask them about where they want to go and speak business language in terms of dollars and percentages and growth.

For example, if you're talking to a CEO, or you're talking to a VP of sales or a VP of marketing and one of their goals is to grow their company from $50 million of revenue to $75 million of revenue, now you have a delta.

You may have another prospect who runs a fast-growth technology startup. They're twenty employees right now, but you hear plans from your buyer that they'd like to grow to a hundred employees because they're going to scale this thing up fast. They're going to take over the world. Now again, you have a metric.

Third example: If they say, hey, we're number 7 in the market and we'd love to be a top-3 firm—and maybe you see this in the business journal, in the news, in an association magazine, or in their annual report—there's a delta. Moving from number 7 to number 3.

How can you as the speaker and as the expert help them accomplish those moves?

Whatever the number, whatever the metrics, here are three magic statements you can use right away:

* ✸ *A big part of this program that we're talking about doing together is helping you build a bridge to $75 million of revenue.*
* ✸ *If I'm hearing you right, what we're doing with this strategic work session is building a bridge to that hundred-person team as quickly and smartly as possible, yes?*
* ✸ *One of the big outcomes from this training is equipping your people to build a bridge to cross over from number 7 in the market to become a top-3 firm. Does that sound right?*

In every sales conversation, you must investigate, dig, probe, diagnose, and uncover until you get your number for the bridge.

Show prospects that you're the connector, you're the pathway, you're the bridge builder that can help get them from where they are to where they want to go.

Don't be afraid of numbers. They love their numbers. They love their goals. They love the delta. They talk about these numbers in meetings all the time. If you're positioned as the shortcut that will get them across the bridge as quickly and safely as possible, they're going to pay you handsomely to build that bridge!

57 WHAT YOUR SALES PIPELINE ISN'T

The definition of your sales pipeline is not how many leads you have.

It's not how many people you're calling.

It's not how many people you need to chase down.

It's not how many emails or LinkedIn messages you're sending.

It is defined by one and only one metric and you want to get your head around this. It's super important.

 @dnewman

Your true sales pipeline is how many people have YOUR name in their calendar.

You're not calling them. They're going to call you.

How many follow-up calls do you have scheduled where your name is in their calendar?

I personally never follow up. I don't call. They call me. This isn't about arrogance or superiority—it's a condition of doing business with a trusted advisor.

When you're sick, you call the doctor. The doctor doesn't call and ask if you're sick! You talk to the doctor on her timeline and her availability to see if she can help you.

Never leave a sales conversation without nailing down the next step on their calendar. You can do this via email, phone, video, whatever method you normally use. Simply say, "Let's put a pushpin on the calendar to discuss our next step; at that time, please call me at 1-888-BEST-SPEAKER-EVER."

Why is this important? Because your status is high. You're a peer not a peddler. No begging. No chasing.

Think about it: If you're a professional speaker or a consultant or an expert of any kind, you are a public figure and a thought-leading expert. Public figures don't chase. Public figures don't beg. Public figures don't call and re-call and hound and follow up. Public figures don't have their email going into a black hole. Public figures don't have their voice mails go unanswered. You're a public figure. You're a rock star. It's time to start selling like one.

 # 58 KILLER SALES QUESTIONS FOR SPEAKERS

Remember, before you can offer a prescription, you want to investigate, diagnose, uncover, and probe; you want to find out what's really going on.

Here are twelve killer sales questions for speakers. Some of these are mine and some I've collected from some of the smartest and most successful speakers that I know in the National Speakers Association.

1. How is the economy affecting your members or employees or attendees? This could be economy is good, economy is bad, economy is flat. It doesn't matter. You want to figure out how they are doing overall. Take an overall health check of how they're doing relative to the economy. Even if you think you know the answers, it's important to ask because they're going to tell you the real deal. You're going to get all kinds of great data and great information from this question.

2. What are they complaining about in the hallways and at the water cooler? You want to find that out too. A great way to uncover pains and frustrations. You're putting your finger on the pulse. What's bugging them? What's making them unhappy? Where are they going off the rails?

3. If you were me, what would you want to know that I couldn't possibly know about this group (or this meeting or this industry or this organization or this issue)? I love this one. This is from my friend Terri Langhans, CSP, and it's a magic question. Because she knows that she's an outsider and the person she's talking to lives there. You will get golden answers to this one.

4. What do these employees or attendees or members fear the most? What are they afraid of? Well, they're afraid of Walmart. They're afraid of disruptive technology. They're afraid of foreign competition. They're afraid of the big merger the company's going through right now. They're afraid of being fired. They're afraid of X, of Y, of Z, and you want to know that. You need to know that.

5. What do these employees or attendees or members want the most? What are their aspirations? What are their hopes? What are their dreams? What are they really wishing for?

6. What do you want your people to think, do, and feel differently after my program? This one's from my friend Dr. Alan Zimmerman, CSP, CPAE, and it's a bull's-eye outcome question. If the answer to that question is "nothing," you're not going to make a sale. This is an "instant on" question that immediately focuses them on—what's the end result? What's the endgame? Is the journey worth the trip? And how can you get them there more quickly and easily?

7. What were you planning to do after the event to help your people with ongoing repetition, reinforcement, and application? This is from my friend Thom Winninger, CSP, CPAE, who says most audiences want something to help them continue the learning after the presentation. There are many options: a copy of your book, digital audio downloads, digital video downloads, a follow-up webinar, follow-up access to you via email or phone, and so on. The magic words here are repetition, reinforcement, application.

8. For you to decide that this program was wildly successful, what would you want to see, hear, or experience for yourself and from your top team? Very insightful question that's going to surface all kinds of wonderful answers. I've heard things like "good bathroom buzz." When I walk into the bathroom, I want people to say, "Oh my gosh, wasn't that great? What a fantastic speaker. What an awesome program. This was the best conference in years and years and years." It could be bathroom buzz. It could be economic impact for their members. It could be kudos from their CEO. It could be any of a dozen different things. You want to find out what the main success signs for them are.

9. Describe previous speakers or programs that were very well received by this group. Ask them what exactly about that program made it so successful and well received. Get as many specifics as you can so you can model on that success.

10. Describe previous speakers or programs that were NOT well received by this group. This will help you understand what to stay away from, reassure them that you don't do, and what to avoid.

11. What else would you like to see from me to help you make your decision? This is a great closing question. This is a trusted advisor posture. You're serving your prospect. You're also going back to that concept of it's a *decision*. Your mind-set should be, "You're going to decide. You're going to share that decision with me so what else would you like to see from me to help you make your decision?"

12. What's the next step in your decisionmaking process? They will tell you, "We have a committee meeting on the twentieth," or "I have to run this by our CEO," or "We have our board meeting next week," so you'll get a timeline, and from that, you can build a reverse timeline to help you establish when to put that pushpin in the calendar to collect their decision and answer any final questions they may have.

Bonus Question: When would it make sense for us to put a pushpin in the calendar to discuss your decision or answer any final questions you may have? Why is that a bonus question? I want to give it to you *again* so that you absolutely start using this question. I'm not sure if it's a million-dollar question, but I've certainly made multiple six figures with this question!

The top 1 percent of speakers, smart speakers, successful speakers, ask these kinds of questions on sales call number 1. I want you to be in that 1 percent of successful speakers who close deal after deal after deal.

59 BE WILLING TO WALK AWAY. *REALLY.*

Please, please be willing to walk away from a bad deal, a cheap prospect, or a client who insists on undervaluing your expertise.

> **@dnewman**
> Some clients are broke. Don't go broke with them.

When you speak for a broke client organization, the spin-off business will be other broke clients.

On the other hand, clients with money will refer you and connect you with other clients that have money—corporations, associations, meeting planners, and conference producers.

Now, can you convert business from a free speech? Absolutely, and you will and you should. Free speaking as a proactive and targeted *lead*-generating strategy: Awesome. Free speaking as a *revenue* strategy: No. Doesn't compute. Stay away!

If they want you bad enough, they will always find the money. Here are two stories, both of which ended up in a full fee program from previously broke people, or at least a good reasonable fee, the fee I wanted to get.

STORY 1:
IT'S REALLY BEAUTIFUL HERE

I did a full day of training for a big nonprofit arts organization. It was at the Four Seasons Hotel in Philadelphia, beautiful room, great food, no expense spared.

The two people who hired me said, *By the way, we're also on the board of our national association. We have a conference coming up in Santa Fe. Can you do the same program for us there that you did here?* I said sure, absolutely. It will be the same program, same fee, same arrangement, that okay? Yes, sure, fine, no problem.

We take this idea to the association's executive director who says, "*Oh, we have no speaker budget. We can't pay you that same fee.*"

I replied, "*Really? Well then we have a problem because if you don't have the fee, then I can't be your speaker.*" I said this verbatim, politely, and then I pivoted into:

ME: *Are there some other creative sources of funding? Is there a sponsor? Is there an exhibitor? Is there a big vendor that always takes out the full-page ad in the program?*

BUYER: *Nope, we've got no money, no speaker budget, no nothing.*

ME: *Well, I'd love to help you but if there's no budget then there's no speaker.*

BUYER: *But it's in Santa Fe. Santa Fe is beautiful. You'll be staying at the beautiful El Dorado Hotel and Spa right in downtown Santa Fe. It's going to be great. In fact, you can bring your wife and kids and stay a couple extra days.*

ME: (laughing) *I appreciate your entrepreneurial spirit, but to be fair to the client who just hired me and referred me to you, I can't do it without the fee.*

I hung up the phone and figured I was never going to hear from them again. A week later, the phone rings . . .

BUYER: *Hi, David, it's Susan from the association—we found the money.*

ME: *Really? Where'd you find the money?*

BUYER: *We have this education fund. It's been sitting there unused, untapped, so we definitely have more than your fee in that education fund. We're going to use some of that education fund to bring you in.*

ME: *Great!*

And I did, in fact, bring my lovely bride. We did bring the kids. We did stay a couple extra days at the El Dorado Hotel (which IS beautiful) and I got my full fee because I was willing to walk away.

STORY 2:
WE FORGOT TO ASK: WHAT'S YOUR NONPROFIT RATE?

Nonprofit organizations love to tell you they're broke, except they have six thousand employees all across the country, they have a state-of-the-art website, they have all this fabulous stuff, they raise money like nobody's business, but they still claim that they're broke.

I remember negotiating with one nonprofit client, and I'm talking to the national director of training and development and things are going well.

* The fee is $X,XXX.
* Super. Here's the date. Here are the logistics. So glad to be working with you.

I send over the paperwork, they sign the paperwork, they return the paperwork: smooth as silk.

Three days after receiving the paperwork, an assistant calls me from the decisionmaker's office:

* Hi, Mr. Newman. I'm calling from Jane's office and I'm so embarrassed. We forgot to ask you, do you have a nonprofit rate?

Cue dramatic music. **Do you have a nonprofit rate?** I must have had enough coffee that day or it was divine intervention because literally without even thinking, I replied, "You're getting my nonprofit rate."

The only piece of data that I did not share is that my nonprofit rate is exactly the same as my for-profit rate.

And yours should be as well.

To get your free video replay of my "Sell More Speaking" master-class training, visit doitmarketing.com/sell.

DO IT! SUCCESS STRATEGY: TURN YOUR CLIENTS INTO VOLUNTEER MARKETERS

BY JAY BAER, CSP, CPAE

Speaking is the best job ever.

Which is why there are more and more and more and more speakers than ever.

Every speaker has to possess their Ts and Cs. It's nonnegotiable. You want to be a speaker? You must have a Terrific Topic and be able to Create Change. Period.

But if you've got that part figured out, the next thing you should be pondering is how to stand out from the herd of speakers trying to get hired.

Word of mouth is the single most important component of speaking success. Among audiences, and even more so among meeting planners and bureaus. Data shows that more than 90 percent of business-to-business (B2B) purchases are influenced by word of mouth. And speaking gigs are all B2B!

This is why it's so unfathomable that, given its importance to the success of a speaking career, very few speakers have an actual word-of-mouth strategy. Instead, most speakers just assume that competency will create conversation. Just give a good speech and meeting planners will talk about you. But why would they?

Human beings are physiologically wired to discuss things that are different, and ignore things that are average.

(continues)

143

Nobody has EVER said: "Hey, let me tell you about this good speaker I heard recently."

You know this to be true. Yet, so many speakers still play follow the leader. They find a speaker they like, whose information and style is kinda/sorta similar, and try to mimic as faithfully as possible. This may work for a little while, but imitation is an express elevator to mediocrity.

What you need is a reliable word-of-mouth strategy that is powered by a Talk Trigger, a consistent differentiator that COMPELS word of mouth. It simply forces audiences and planners to tell others about you, and how you are different and memorable.

There are five different types of Talk Triggers. I break them all down in my bestselling book by the same name. The book also includes dozens of examples, a six-step process you can (and should) use to figure out your own Talk Trigger, a quick reference guide, and some word-of-mouth surprises, too, of course.

I'll break down the five types of triggers for you here, and give you examples of speakers that epitomize each of them, to give you some ideas.

But remember, Same Is Lame.

Don't copy these; read the book and figure out your own word-of-mouth strategy.

1. Talkable Generosity: This is the type of Talk Trigger most often seen, as it's the easiest to think through and implement. It's when you are more generous than your customers expect. And a lot of speakers already give their clients thank-you gifts and such, but how could you put a little twist on it?

Shep Hyken does this by gifting his clients beautiful carving knives. But not with Shep's logo on them . . . with the client's logo on them!

Speaker and author John Ruhlin says that a gift with your logo on it isn't a gift, it's an advertisement. Shep puts a twist on the gift and makes it talkable by personalizing it for the recipient.

2. Talkable Usefulness: This is when you're more useful than your clients expect. Andrew Davis is the master at this approach. After every event, he sends the meeting planner a list of speakers he recommends, in every major speaking category. Brilliant.

3. Talkable Responsiveness: This is when you're faster and more on top of it than your clients anticipate. Eagles Talent Speakers Bureau does this, promising same-day response when you request information on their website. Especially now, when lead times for speaker selection seems to be shrinking fast, promising a quick answer on price and availability is very smart, and noticeable.

4. Talkable Empathy: This is one that wouldn't have made the list two years ago, but we certainly find ourselves—in business, in life, and certainly in politics—in an empathy deficit these days. This may be disheartening, but it's a real opportunity, because when you can be warm, and human, and caring today it STANDS OUT like never before.

Who is the unsung hero of events where you speak? The AV team, every time.

Here's what I do; it's one of my own Talk Triggers. I get custom Amazon gift cards printed with my logo, and I give them to every AV person backstage, at every event.

Yes, audiences and meeting planners talk. But so does the AV team!

5. Talkable Attitude: This is when you're just a little bit DIFFERENT than the other speaker. Quirky, even. This one is the most fun, but perhaps the hardest to pull off because many speakers are a little wacky, which is why they're speakers.

My favorite speaker example of talkable attitude is social justice speaker Jess Pettit. She has two superpowers: She's an amazing speaker, and she knows how to perfectly fold a fitted bedsheet. You know, the troublesome ones with the elastic corners?

(continues)

When someone fills out the inquiry form on her website, they instantly receive an email with a link to a four-minute video of Jess demonstrating her exceptional fitted bedsheet skills. The last line of the video clinches it:

"You've seen her fold a fitted sheet. Imagine what she can do for your next event."

See what I mean? Same Is Lame. We discuss different, and ignore average. In the hypercompetitive speaking business, you simply must have a terrific topic that can create change. But you better have a word-of-mouth strategy, as well.

Get started on your Talk Trigger now and get those client conversations rolling!

Jay Baer, CSP, CPAE, is a seventh-generation entrepreneur, the bestselling author of six books, and a founder of five multimillion-dollar companies. A Hall of Fame keynote speaker and emcee, Jay is the founder of Convince & Convert, a consulting firm that helps the world's most iconic brands gain and keep more customers through the smart use of marketing, customer service, and word of mouth.

60 FIVE STRATEGIES FOR CORPORATE EXECUTIVES TO GET MORE FROM EVERY SPEAKING GIG

Executive speaking engagements at industry con-ferences, trade shows, association meetings, and public-facing events are a vital part of your strategic marketing, sales, and business development arsenal BUT . . .

Most companies don't have an optimized speaking strategy for their top executives.

You're already investing hundreds of thousands of dollars (or more) in sending your executives, sales leaders, and brand/product managers to speak at industry events, trade shows, and meetings.

You want your people to bring home the bacon. In this case, bacon isn't a tasty pork product—it's more demos, more meetings, more appointments, and more closed deals.

You already know that executives who speak win more business . . . but how do you make sure your team's speaking efforts consistently pay off and are worthy of the financial and non-financial investment (time, travel, resources, opportunity cost) you're making?

These five strategies are part of what we teach in our "Executive Speaker Branding" program to large companies and their marketing, sales, and leadership teams.

See how many of these five areas are optimized for your executives—and which ones you could use some help with:

1. Content—I'm just going to say it. Most "canned" corporate presentations are dull, boring, and non-compelling. They've gone through so many revisions and so many people's hands that all energy, humor, and cleverness have been removed. Those have been dutifully replaced with the lowest common denominator "vanilla" flavoring to make sure they are 100 percent standardized, current, compliant, and kosher. When we're invited to work with a team on improving their presentation content, we never throw the baby out with the bathwater, but we DO start with a clean slate and as we create, improve, and rebuild, we require that every idea/slide point/story "audition" its way back in with one central question as the filter: WHY is this content needed—in other words, what's the optimal outcome of sharing it?

2.   **Relevance**—Even valuable, informative, and well-delivered content is going to land flat if it's not immediately relevant to the audience you're addressing. Every presentation cannot be delivered in the same way to different audiences when you and your company have different outcomes in mind for those audiences. Increasing the relevance factor in your presentations means strategically tailoring the content (adding, deleting, changing key vocabulary) and making sure you know your audience ahead of time. We often recommend (and meeting planners love) doing a "needs and interests" survey a few months before the event to gauge that particular audience's most relevant needs, wants, and desires. Rather than improving your relevance with guessing, improve it with data.

3.   **Persuasion Architecture®**—We teach our corporate clients a proven speaking formula called Persuasion Architecture® that has been used in direct marketing, advertising, TV commercials, and online for decades. This is the "missing piece" in almost all corporate presentations we see. There's no intentional "buildup" in most presentations—yes, even most sales presentations—that leads your audience through a journey of self-discovery to the fact that they need to TAKE ACTION on what you're presenting. Our clients get radically different results the moment we help them change this one aspect of their presentation content and delivery. It is the key to building a results-focused presentation that compels your audience to act: Buy. Sign up. Get a demo. Book a call.

4.   **Calls to action**—This may seem obvious but let's stay on the track of those actions I just mentioned: Buy. Sign up. Get a demo. Book a call. I'd like you to guess right now how many presentations we see where there

is NO call to action—NO explicit mention of what the speaker would like the audience to DO—either right then and there in the meeting room, or on their phones, or out in the trade show exhibit area, or anywhere and anytime. The number is 80 percent. That means that only 20 percent of the time before we work with a client are they even ASKING for the desired outcome that they want from that event after spending (wasting?) all that time, energy, money, and preparation. As in life, you'll always drastically improve the chances of getting what you want if you clearly and repeatedly ASK for it!

5.   **Practice**—Here's the low-hanging fruit. Every C-suite executive, sales leader, and brand/product manager can instantly get better at their speaking presentations if they practice. But all practice is not created equal. You must LEARN to practice (weird, right?). The first big surprise for most of our clients is that practice does not mean "practice in your head" or even mutter the words under your breath as you flip through your slides sitting at your desk. Close your door. Stand up. Get your remote clicker. Practice out loud—full voice—and with intentional movement just as you would when you're live onstage in front of a few hundred people. Practice includes pausing for audience reactions, making smooth transitions from one part of your talk to the next, refining your stories (using fewer words and more cinematic story techniques)—and it's especially important to practice your customized language, references, and success stories to THAT audience, for THAT industry, and in THAT moment in time. (Sad truth: You can practice this way even with your current crappy presentations and they'll improve significantly. Not as much as if you completely overhaul them with points 1 to 4 above, but hey, it's better than nothing!)

Every time any of your executives go out to speak, if those prospects and audiences don't immediately "get it, need it, and want it"—and if you're not triggering urgency to act—you're losing opportunities, wasting time, and missing sales.

Once you sharpen your skills in these five vital areas, you'll get a more consistent flow of leads, customers, and cash. That's how smart leaders at top companies consistently get more out of every speaking gig.

61 SEVEN BUILDING BLOCKS OF EXECUTIVE SPEAKING SUCCESS

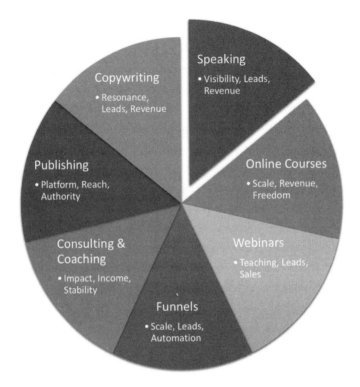

Pie chart with the following segments:

- **Speaking** — • Visibility, Leads, Revenue
- **Online Courses** — • Scale, Revenue, Freedom
- **Webinars** — • Teaching, Leads, Sales
- **Funnels** — • Scale, Leads, Automation
- **Consulting & Coaching** — • Impact, Income, Stability
- **Publishing** — • Platform, Reach, Authority
- **Copywriting** — • Resonance, Leads, Revenue

Questions I get from C-suite executives and corporate leaders who speak:

✳ David, what does it take to **gain preeminence** in my market?

✳ How can I become the **go-to person** in my topic/niche?

✳ How can I **expand my reach**, grow my list, and build my platform?

* What can I offer my audiences **after I speak** to stay top of mind?
* How do I build **marketing magnetism** for my speeches, so I get more gigs?
* I speak a lot for my company/brand, but why am I not **seeing enough results**?

All these questions have their answers **hidden in one of seven key areas** of your thought-leadership strategy as an executive or professional who speaks . . .

Here's the full picture of all seven building blocks you need:

Let's explore each one—and see how you can tune, tweak, and improve anything that's missing, not performing, or could use a major overhaul in YOUR world . . .

1. Speaking—Obviously, this is my area of expertise. Having a solid speaker marketing strategy is vital to help you gain visibility in front of audiences who matter (that is, buyers and decisionmakers); generate leads for your products, services, and programs; and generate revenue and respect via speaking fees for your executive and leaders. Speaking is one of the most powerful lead-generators and revenue-generators in your expertise-driven business.

But how do you scale this above and beyond the audiences that you can reach through live speaking? The next pie slice has your answer . . .

2. Online Courses—The most successful experts, speakers, and consultants are embracing the power of online courses, e-learning, and digital distribution methods for their expertise. The first benefit here is pure scalability—your business can reach thousands (or tens of thousands) of ideal customers, prospects, and buyers through the power of online courses. As a source of revenue, online courses are hard to beat because you create it once and get paid over and over and over. This allows you to create a high-value thought-leadership asset that is no longer tied to your personal time, attention, and presence. Jackpot!!

But now how do you reach those thousands of eager prospects, buyers, and decisionmakers? Let's look at the next piece of the pie . . .

3. Webinars—The day I fully embraced webinar marketing back in 2012, my entire business—heck, my entire life—changed dramatically. We are living in an "Attention Economy"—meaning, when it comes to getting more business from your crazy-busy buyers, you first need to earn their attention and only then do you get the chance to earn their money! The #1 best way to deliver massive value to your subscribers, fans, followers, and prospects is with content-rich webinars that teach actionable strategies, tactics, and tools. You need to be radically helpful and radically generous. This is what converts strangers to friends and friends to prospects and prospects to paying customers who love you, buy, repeat, recommend, and refer like crazy.

But webinars presented here and there sporadically and without a clear strategy are not going to do the trick. So you need . . .

4. Funnels—A marketing funnel is simply a fancy word for a programmatic sequence of touchpoints—emails, videos, blog posts, webinars, PDFs, and other helpful communications—delivered in a specific sequence to a specific subset of people specifically interested in a certain one of your products, services, or programs. A marketing funnel is your lifeline that keeps you connected to prospects who are at various phases of the buying cycle—from merely interested in the topic (browsers) all the way to committed to investing in your solutions/services (buyers). A well-designed marketing funnel will take a cold lead from initial contact to signed contract in a predetermined sequence designed to both add value and extend offers and invitations to your relevant investable opportunities. Without a marketing funnel in place, you risk alienating prospects who are NOT interested in buying today while completely missing out on sales to the hot prospects who are ready to buy right now.

But what about long-term stability and predictable revenue? The best way to share your expertise and gain this benefit is . . .

5. Consulting/Coaching—Having longer-term engagements on your service menu—such as ninety-day coaching packages or year-long consulting programs or monthly facilitated mastermind roundtables—is a great way to increase your impact on client results. Remember, people don't really value transactions—but they VERY much value programs and services that deliver transformation. And delivering results over a sustained period of time is the best way to guarantee your clients' success. Because of the greater depth, breadth, and duration of these engagements, it is much easier to get premium fees from premium clients who are deeply committed to the transformation you offer that will get them the results they truly want. These longer-term engagements also provide the foundation of your financial stability because the income is significant and ongoing.

But then how do you capture "lightning in a bottle" to let all the folks who can't afford your consulting or coaching know you are the real-deal resource who can help them when they're ready to transform?

6. **Publishing**—One of the best ways to do this is with publishing a non-fiction business book based on the expertise you already have. Writing, publishing, and promoting a business book that captures your methodology, training, and tools is an outstanding way to build your platform, expand your reach, and establish your authority as the go-to expert in your specific topic, niche, or industry. After all, you "wrote the book" on it so you must be a highly credible expert. And—some tough love coming up here—your book needs to be excellent. Not just good or very good, but truly great. It does NOT need to be long—in fact, the bestselling business books of all time are less than 120 pages in a small five-by-seven trade publishing format. But just writing a book for the sake of having a book (and a crappy one at that) is definitely not going to help promote your expertise. That's why the book needs to be marketed, launched, and sold for the long-term impact it can have on your professional success.

And what makes all of these components really take off? It's about how you articulate and distinguish them with your messaging and packaging, which means you need to master . . .

7. **Copywriting**—To clear up any confusion, copywriting has nothing to do with patents, trademarks, and copyright notices! "Copy" is written content designed to persuade or sell. Copywriting is one of the most essential elements of effective marketing and successful selling. It is the art and science of strategically delivering words (whether written or spoken) that get people to take some form of action. Good copy resonates with the reader and is relevant, valuable, attractive, and effective in communicating the value, impact, results, outcomes, and emotional payoffs tied to investing in and benefiting from your products, services, or programs. The better you are at copywriting, the more prospects, leads, and sales you will generate because you'll be able to quickly get your prospects to "get it, need it, and want it" when considering buying from you.

Master these seven areas and you'll have everything in place for your global speaker domination!

DO IT! SUCCESS STRATEGY: WHY EVERY SPEAKER NEEDS A BOOK

BY DAN JANAL

If you want to be a highly paid speaker, then you'll need a book as much as you'll need a microphone, a stage, and a spotlight.

Like a microphone, a book helps you share your message, show your brilliance, and explain your ideas so you can help the world become a better place.

Like a stage, a book elevates your position—literally and figuratively—so you stand above other speakers and so that audiences see you as the expert and authority you are.

Like a spotlight, a book shines a light on you, so the audience gets to see who you really are. A good book helps people get to know, like, and trust you so they will hire you. The light emanating from your book helps prospects realize you are the trusted guide who can lead them from their mess into success.

In fact, if you haven't written a book, you will lose jobs to speakers who have written books. Having written one book is the minimum entry point for a highly paid speaker.

No doubt, you've seen many bright, shiny objects that could help you market your speaking career and business. However, none do the job as well as a book.

A book gives you the opportunity to showcase the products and services you can offer to help them solve their problems. You can tell fascinating case-study stories of how you saved your clients. Your book is your silent salesperson that can make money by providing order forms, call-to-action statements, and a simple "contact us" page.

Finally, a book is a cash register. Your book makes money for you: via product sales when you speak, on Amazon, and on your webpage.

Here's a fact that only the savviest speakers know: Speakers use books as a way to "sweeten the deal" to get speaking engagements. For example, an organization could not afford to hire you. However, they might have an education budget or a training budget that will let them buy thousands of dollars of books. If you bundle your speaking fee with your book sales, you could create a superb payday!

While many big-name speakers have their names on books, they also have a secret: Many didn't write their books. They hired a ghostwriter to turn their speeches, their blogs, and their thoughts into a book that propels the speaker's career and bank account.

Why would a speaker hire a ghostwriter? Reasons include:

1. They are too busy to write a book because they are traveling and speaking so often.

2. Gifted speakers might not be gifted writers. They can't spell, don't know proper grammar, or aren't disciplined to put in the long hours needed to write a book.

3. Ken Blanchard, the bestselling author of over sixty books including *The One-Minute Manager* and *Who Moved My Cheese?*, told me he writes all of his books with a coauthor because he always learns from other people.

(continues)

Isn't it time you thought about the book you need to write—or have written for you—so you can give your speaking business the boost it needs so you can help even more people?

Dan Janal *is called the Michelangelo of book editors, book coaches, and ghostwriters because he sculpts your material into a masterpiece. For information, go to WriteYourBookInAFlash.com.*

62 HOW THE TED TALKS CRAZE HAS CHANGED BUSINESS CONFERENCES

Nothing has changed the world of public speaking

in the last few decades like the TED talk phenomenon. Because of the popularity of TED talks, the self-appointed speech police may think that the TED format is *the* only way to present a speech. Watch out for negative feedback if you don't follow the "rules."

 @dnewman

Be prepared to get requests for TED-style talks from clients who don't know what that means.

WHAT IS A TED TALK?

TED stands for "Technology, Entertainment, and Design," and their tagline is "Ideas Worth Spreading." The TED organization is a nonprofit that has been hosting speaking conferences since 1984. The maximum speech length is eighteen minutes and speakers are not paid. Their content rules are: "no political agendas, no religious proselytizing, and only good science." They focus on "structure, brevity, and purpose" and connecting with the audience.

WHAT BUSINESS
SPEAKERS NEED TO KNOW

The TED format, emotional style, and mystique are so pervasive that they can affect how your speeches are perceived. The format should be discussed with clients to avoid unrealistic expectations. Consider discussing it, briefly, with your audience. There is nothing wrong with stating, "I know TED talks are popular and I'd love to do one now but I have a lot of valuable information to share with you and more content than will fit into eighteen minutes."

You must decide how the TED style, format, and length works (or doesn't) for your topic and clients, on a case-by-case basis. But you can always be a more interesting and engaging speaker. Why not watch some of the most popular and least popular TED talks; you will learn something from each speaker. You can ask questions of your audience and create experiences. Remember: Nobody wants to listen to a droning talking-head speaker.

A MATTER OF TIME

The TED time limit is perfect for telling an emotional story of a pivotal life moment or a basic feel-good concept. However, if you are presenting quantitative or technical information, additional time will be needed. If you are presenting at a training course, especially a continuing education session, eighteen minutes won't cut it with an accreditation board.

If you are the keynote speaker at an expensive conference, with an hour or two-hour time slot, and you sit down after only eighteen minutes, I guarantee that there will be hell to pay. Even if you were directly asked to do a TED-style talk. Once something becomes part of the social culture, people often toss around terms with no idea of the meaning. So never assume that the event coordinator requesting a TED talk is asking for eighteen minutes maximum. You always need to make sure everyone is on the same page.

An option is to do an interactive and brief TED-type talk in the afternoon, after lunch when people tend to get drowsy. It can be the perfect way to introduce a topic that will be discussed in depth later in the conference or to reinforce an earlier presentation.

DO WHAT WORKS FOR YOU AND ENGAGE YOUR AUDIENCE

The short and emotional storytelling TED format works really well in some forums and not others. Yes, the cool kids are using the TED style, but you have to look at each situation and determine if it works for the specific venue. Ultimately, most conferences aren't looking for eighteen minutes, but they want the emotion and the engagement of a TED-style talk. People remember how you make them feel. If you create that TED-type of connection with your audience, you'll have a successful event.

 63 SHORT-TALK VENUE SUMMARIES

In our short-attention-span world, it should come as no surprise that short length format talks are all the rage. From the long-standing granddaddy of the short format, "TED talks," which have been around for decades, to the newer and much shorter PechaKucha and Ignite Talks, it seems like long speeches will soon be long gone.

> **@dnewman**
> Don't get sucked in by TED. Longer talks will always have a place in the world of business speaking.

But you would be wise to refine your speaking skills by trying out these short formats and learning from their strengths and weaknesses. Each of the major speaking forums and formats has their own unique culture, vision, mission, etc. Some are very polished, some are very emotional; some are artsy, while others are focused.

Creative Mornings breakfast talks are built around a loose format-free breakfast, a medium-length talk (twenty to thirty minutes), questions, and networking. Free coffee and free hugs. Started in 2008 in New York City as a venue for creatives to meet for a talk and free breakfast, it has expanded to nearly two hundred cities all over the world. And it has recently morphed into the Creative Guild, an international online membership network. Their speakers appear to be much more free-form, artsy, and less polished. Their mission: "We believe in giving a damn. We believe in face-to-face connections, in learning from others, in hugs and high-fives."

In stark contrast to Creative Mornings, **TED talks** are very polished, focused, and business-oriented even if they are dealing with emotional subjects. As I mention above, TED signifies "Technology, Entertainment, and Design." Started in 1984 with annual idea conferences, the TED foundation is a major player in the hip influencer culture and for a long time was a very elite group. In the last decade, it has become accessible with a multitude of talks available online. And the rank and file can now attend a number of regional TED forum spin-offs called TEDx. The talks are short on length and long on emotion. The maximum speech time is eighteen minutes and the organizers make sure that the speakers are well prepared and focused.

PopTech is a newer and a bit less glamorous version of TED. They, too, hold an annual idea conference, with ten- to twenty-minute talks, which are filmed and shared online. They feel "the role of a speaker is to instigate and inspire emerging bodies of work and next chapters in life—either collaboratively or as individuals." Their focus is on technology as well as art and social change.

Lightning talks are extremely short format talks with very strict rules. The two most common are PechaKucha and Ignite Talks. PechaKucha is a microtalk style that has a very rigid format: Twenty slides, twenty seconds per slide, for a total of six minutes and forty seconds. It requires honing down your topic to the bare essentials and having everything perfectly timed. Because the slides advance automatically every twenty seconds, if you don't have your presentation rehearsed, it can be a real mess. The Ignite format is very similar to that of PechaKucha but even shorter. The rules are twenty slides, fifteen seconds per preloaded slide, for a total speaking time of only five minutes!

What to learn from these short formats? People want information packaged in easy-to-take-in, bite-size amounts. They want to discuss ideas and interact with presenters. People want engaging, inspiring content that is well prepared and focused. They want you to share your passion.

64 YOUR THREE MAIN GOALS IN A SHORT TALK

When you present a short talk, twenty minutes or less, you need to quickly entertain, engage, and motivate your audience.

@dnewman

Your goals for a short talk: Make them laugh, make them think, make them act.

People no longer have any patience for "talking heads" that lecture at them rather than talk with them.

All these principles can be applied to a presentation of any length.

Good speaking is not dependent on the style, format, or time frame of your talk.

HUMOR THEM

One of the best ways to entertain and educate an audience is by adding humor to your talk. People remember how you make them feel, and if you get them to smile or laugh, you immediately create a connection. Start by smiling at them, which will help them feel more comfortable and at ease. Tell an interesting story or discuss an unusual observation rather than trying to be a stand-up comedian. If you aren't sure about your comedic talents, be sure to test out your talk with family, friends, or colleagues.

KNOW THEM

Knowing who your audience is, what they are interested in, and what they want to learn from you is critical, whether you are speaking for five minutes or two days.

Remember, effective speakers work with their audience and tailor their subject to their audience. Talks should not be one-size-fits-all. Audiences recognize and appreciate customized content.

POLL THEM

An easy way to connect with and engage a group is by asking them questions and making them think. This can be done simply by posing questions and having people respond back. Or you can use an online polling service to post questions and allow the audience to reply on their phones. You can design your own poll or game or use a polling platform. The aggregated response results can be integrated into your PowerPoint or other presentations for extra engagement. This tool can be used for icebreaking or community-building games or training. It can also be used to allow your audience to ask you questions.

MOVE THEM

While you only have a few minutes to speak, you definitely have ample time to motivate your audience to take action. Your short talk can be the perfect vehicle to get the group excited about your book or your longer speeches. It can also move them to improve their own results and be braver in making changes in their own lives, businesses, and careers.

KISS—KEEP IT SIMPLE, SPEAKER!

This old standby is still valuable advice especially for short-talk formats. It is so important to distill your topic down to just a few essential elements and points when doing a short talk. You cannot just talk really fast (seriously, people have tried it) and call it a TED talk. In fact, you often need to slow down, take a deep breath, and curb the urge to rush when you only have a short time to speak.

@dnewman

In a short talk, content is not your friend. Go for impact, not volume!

PRACTICE, PRACTICE, PRACTICE

Speaking in a short-talk format leaves no room for fluff or flying by the seat of one's pants. You don't have to have every second choreographed if that isn't your style, but this format does require greater discipline and preparation than an hour-long keynote speech. Don't get cocky because it is a topic you've spoken on numerous times or the short style will beat you. It is definitely a different endeavor, but if handled correctly, it can hone your speaking skills in a way you'll never get from giving a long speech.

65 AVOIDING DEATH BY POWERPOINT

PowerPoint presentations or slides have become such an expected part of business speeches and other talks that many people think they are mandatory for every talk. If you mention that you are doing a speech without PowerPoint, people will probably look at you like you are from Mars. This is because they don't recall that pleasant time, in the past, when people actually talked with audiences instead of narrating a slideshow. PowerPoint can be used to share truly memorable images, or it can create mind-numbing boredom. Please use your PowerPoint tools for good, not evil!

DEATH BY POWERPOINT

Thinking that PowerPoint must be used in every talk has led to slides being used for the sake of having slides rather than because they enhance the talk. This careless use of slides has led to too many torturous sessions, a veritable "death by a thousand slides." Based on the large number of Death by PowerPoint memes you can find in a quick Google search, this is becoming a real crisis. Ironically, you can watch several slideshows to allegedly learn how to be a better PowerPointer.

 @dnewman

One of the deadliest PowerPoint sins is putting too many words on each slide.

A SPEAKER OF FEW WORDS

This is often followed by the dreaded reading of said words by the speaker. Speakers often rely too heavily upon their slides to tell their story instead of using their words. And then they use both and then compound the damage by reading the text, which is boring and repetitive. Another problem related to too much text is that it is not readable. It is pointless and annoying to share a slide that most of the audience can't actually read.

SHOWCASE IMPORTANT POINTS

One of the benefits of using or at least trying out some of the popular short-talk formats is that you are forced to focus and refine your ideas down to the essential elements. You should do the same for the content of each and every PowerPoint slide you use. Get rid of all those multiple bullet points (deadly). And delete those busy charts and graphs; again, they are generally unreadable. Fight the urge to fill the space on the screen. It is better to add another slide than to cram too much info onto one slide.

SHARE UNIQUE IMAGES

Don't use your slides to share information that you are able to tell your audience, especially as you are now avoiding reading slides. Instead, use creative and interesting image slides to illustrate your unique stories and content. Your audience doesn't want to see the same images that they've seen in other talks or that they can find easily in a search. Give them unique content—take your own pictures, share your own experiences. Another benefit will be that by using your own images, you will be more engaged and that will translate to your audience. Don't forget the maxim: "A picture is worth a thousand words" IF it is the right image. And again, editing and refining are just as important in reference to image slides as in text slides.

USE SLIDES SPARINGLY AND EFFECTIVELY

Don't use slides to fill time; that is a deadly and lazy practice. Use slides thoughtfully for two important purposes: to reinforce important points and to share unique images. If you are telling a story about a beautiful sunset, by all means, show them the image.

@dnewman

Please use your PowerPoint skills for good, not evil. We've lost too many good speakers that way already!

66 EIGHT KEYS TO GIVING A GREAT SPEECH

1. **Prepare your content.** Giving a great speech begins with what you do before the speech. The first step is writing a speech that is carefully constructed—with a clear beginning that grabs the audience, a middle that hits the core of the argument, and a close that leads to a call for action. Don't assume that you "know your stuff" and will be able to talk extensively about the topic. This is not a cocktail party, in which you can informally present your information. Any signs that you are unprepared or ill-prepared will drain your credibility.

2. **Open strong.** As I explain in the next section, most gun-shy audiences are going to be wary of facing a CEO or executive speaker. They've sat through many boring speeches before, and they have little hope for yours.

Opening strong, with a great story, a humorous but highly relevant joke, a compelling statistic, or even a moving poem that brings the audience in is key. Surprise them, and you will get their attention.

3. **Learn and use key speaking techniques.** Speechwriters have techniques to make the speeches they write more compelling. Here are a few from Richard Dowis, author of *The Lost Art of the Great Speech*:

> **The rule of three.** The Declaration of Independence lists the unalienable rights given by the creator as "life, liberty and the pursuit of happiness." Imagine if Jefferson had written, "life, liberty, the pursuit of happiness, the comfort of family, and a sense of belonging." Just doesn't have the same punch, the same rhythm. The rule of three works: Use it.

> **Repetition.** Especially a few succinct words at the beginning of phrases or sentences. The official term for this technique is anaphora. Martin Luther King Jr. used anaphora brilliantly—it's called the "I Have a Dream" speech for a reason.

> **Hyperbole and understatement.** An obvious exaggeration gets the audience's attention. But understatement can be memorable as well, as this quote from Senator Everett Dirksen demonstrates: "A billion here. A billion there. Pretty soon it adds up to real money."

> **Transitions.** When you write a book like mine, with its intentional microchapters to keep you engaged and moving forward, transitions aren't a big problem. But any other kind of writing, including speeches, needs transitions, if you don't want to sound choppy (and ill-prepared).

> **Antithesis.** This is juxtaposing two sentences or phrases with opposite meanings. No moon chatter is more memorable than Neil Armstrong's "one small step for man, one giant leap for mankind."

4. **Keep it clear and concise.** Forget the big words. Forget the jargon. And please forget the clichés. Check your speech for any confusing statements or thoughts, or any explanations or examples that go on too long. Watch out for passages that are passive or muddled. If you're using brief notes, you'll need to do this editing (and keep doing it) when you're practicing . . . which is what I talk about next.

5. **Practice.** Once you have your speech written or your notes created, it's time to practice. Not in your car. Not in your mind. In real time and real voice. Speak as you will be speaking. Stand as you will be standing. A speech is a performance, and all performances need rehearsals—lots of them. Most of us keep notes in front of us as reminders, but they are only prompts: The more you look at the audience, the more engaged they will be with what you're saying. That means no reading. If you're reading, you're engaged with your paper or the laptop, while the audience mentally (and sometimes physically) leaves.

6. **Watch your body language.** As you are speaking, stand up straight and look into the eyes of the audience. No matter what you are feeling inside, you show the audience that you are unafraid, you are confident, and you are committed to and interested in *them*. Bad posture, head down, eyes glued on page or laptop, frozen statue-like in the same stationary position will send the message that your speech is about you, not them—the fastest way to disengage your audience.

7. **Project and articulate.** If you mumble, if you speak too softly, if you speak too fast, the audience will have a hard time hearing what you're saying—but that's okay, because they won't care! The audience is not going to work to try to hear you. Speak clearly and with enough volume to convey confidence and expertise.

8. **End with a call to action.** "Okay, you've heard me speak, you can go now." Is that really how you want to end? If so, chances are your words are already starting to fade from the consciousness of the audience members as they leave the auditorium. Here's a better idea: Give them something, or a list of things, to do. Tell them how to change their behavior when they get back to the office. Tell them what lessons to keep in mind for the future. A call to action is a marketing term, but after all, are you not selling something in your speech? A new mind-set? New priorities? New motivations? That's why you might close with something like this: *If your employees are disengaged, it's not about them, it's about you. What are you going to do to change their attitudes? Thank you very much.*

67 HOW TO PUT THE WOW IN THE START OF YOUR SPEECH

Let's face it. Unless you're a movie star or come-dian, or a politician from your favorite political party (pick one, I have no opinion on the matter), chances are that even if your audience might be somewhat interested in what you have to say, you can lose them real fast.

Because most of us have sat through so many tortuous speeches—in which the speaker drones on and on as our eyes slowly glaze over and our minds circle the room like trapped bats looking for an escape hatch—any expectations that you, as a CEO or corporate executive, are going to give a compelling, memorable speech are very low. Extremely low. I'm talking Mariana-Trench-deepest-part-of-the-ocean low.

And when expectations are that low, here's what happens: People fully expect you to confirm those expectations, and in fact, they're waiting for you to confirm those expectations! So if you start slow, most of those in the audience are going to think, *yep, a snoozer,* and their minds will tune out and start looking for that escape hatch (*maybe we rent an RV this summer instead of the usual cruise, and I've got to get new shoes, these are way too scuffed . . .*)

If all that sounds scary, it shouldn't, because low expectations actually present you with a great opportunity. Start your speech strong and you'll surprise the hell out of your audience: *Wait a second, this speaker might actually be good!*

How do you start a speech with a wake-up, whiz-banger of an opening?

You've probably heard the advice, start with a joke. Were you the class ham in college? Do you usually have your family and friends in side-holding, tears-flowing stitches at parties and gatherings? Did your wife or husband fall in love with you because of your sense of humor? If you answered "no" or "not even close" to the above, then don't start with a joke. Because the audience knows that they're watching an instruction-sheet speaker (step one: start with a joke).

Now if you do have a sense of humor, sure, use it, with a QUICK humorous comment to break the ice. Bill Clinton once came onstage after a presentation by Benjamin Zander, an orchestra conductor who uses a grand piano and stories from the music world to support his motivational speeches. Zander is wildly exuberant, a talented musician and a very funny man who had the audience simultaneously roaring with laughter while being awed by his beautiful piano playing. As the next speaker, Clinton, the former president of the United States of America, the undisputed star of the lineup that night, and someone known for being a good speaker, came onstage and said with mock concern, "How do you follow that?!"

On the other hand, if you are known for being a bit wooden, you can actually use that to your humor advantage by telling a VERY FUNNY joke. It has to be very funny, so that people laugh out loud while thinking, *Wow, I didn't expect him to be funny!*

But not all speeches need to start with humor. There are other ways to grab their attention.

Maybe you're not funny, no matter what. Or maybe the speech is a very serious speech about a very serious matter, and any humor would be misplaced. There are other ways to start a speech besides the humorous icebreaker, while still grabbing the audience's attention and sending the message that this speech isn't going to be boring.

Here are some other opening ideas:

Statistics. Imagine that a speaker comes to the podium, waits for the polite clapping to peter out, and says, "Every ninety minutes . . . a US veteran commits suicide. Every ninety minutes. And we can do something about it." That's a sobering (and sadly accurate) statistic, and the audience is no longer thinking about what they will have for dinner. Because you've grabbed their attention.

A good story. A truly exceptional and moving story can also be a compelling way to launch your speech. If you're going to tell a story, however, make sure that there's a theme or an obvious lesson to draw from the story. It's very funny that you got lost on Cape Cod and your Kia Soul got stuck on the access road to a private beach for an enclave of mansions, blocking the path of some very rich but very agitated multimillionaires for hours—but what's the point? And even if your story is better than "what I did last summer," keep it short! Otherwise, you may have a surprise ending, but the audience would have tuned out by then.

A quote. A quote can get your audience's attention as long as it's something they haven't heard, and it's truly relevant to the topic of the speech. John F. Kennedy's "Ask not what your country can do for you, ask what you can do for your country," has been done multiple times, and so has his brother's: "Some men see things as they are, and ask why. I dream of things that never were, and ask why not."

If you're going to use a quote, find one that surprises your audience. Here's an example of how a speech using quotes could start:

"Everyone wants to have done more things in their lives. [Being] a schoolteacher would have been very gratifying, I'm sure." *The person who said that is none other than Mick Jagger. Jagger talks about being a rock star like this:* "It is a slightly intellectually undemanding thing to do, being a rock singer, but, you know, you make the best of it." *Well, Mick, I don't agree. If you really want to do more with your life . . . Mick Jagger . . . you can do better than just make the best of it. And that's what we're going to talk about today. Too many of our employees, stuck in jobs that are even less intellectually demanding than being a rock star, are just making the best of it . . .* (You can return to this opening at the end of the speech, by explaining that you have to go . . . Mick Jagger's on the line.)

Poetry. That's not a typo. After all, who reads poetry today, right? So quoting a compelling piece of poetry, linked directly, of course, to the topic of your speech, can surprise and engage your audience. But as with quotes, forget the "how many ways do I love thee" or "a rose is a rose is rose" standards. Surprise them. Move them. Perhaps start with a stanza from a Longfellow poem:

> **Lives of great men all remind us**
> **We can make our lives sublime,**
> **And, departing, leave behind us**
> **Footprints on the sands of time;—**

Then continue: "As CEOs and business leaders, most of us don't think of our lives as 'sublime.' But do we not work every day to make a difference in the world, do we not hope that in our own little way, we will leave footprints in the sands of time? Imagine instilling that spirit in the hearts of your employees . . ."

Whatever choice you make for your opening, practice it over and over again. Don't stumble on the poem's words, don't get lost in your story, don't misquote the quote. Remember: The audience has low expectations, so prove them wrong. Find something new and compelling to get their attention—then make sure you execute flawlessly!

68 MEASURING THE EFFECTIVENESS OF YOUR SPEAKING PROGRAM

 @dnewman

Most companies don't have an effective speaking strategy for their executives.

Imagine playing a game every day—for money—
and not knowing all the rules . . .

Problem: Seeking and responding to executive speaking opportunities blind to ROI, based on a senior executive's vacation schedule, or where the CEO likes to play golf (no, I'm not kidding).

Bigger problem: Spending tens (or hundreds) of thousands of dollars sending your senior leaders, marketing and sales executives, brand managers, and others to speak at trade shows, conferences, and key industry events . . . yet never knowing what worked, what didn't, or how to improve for next time.

There has to be a better way . . . and now there is.

Most organizations have never focused on the growing need to systematically maximize the value of their industry experts who speak at conferences and to the media.

The demand for executives such as your Chief Sustainability Officer, CFO, CMO, CIO/CTO, and other thought-leading executives on the speaking circuit highlights the value of an "all-hands-on-deck" approach to developing your speaker bench strength.

Once you've mastered your executive speaking platform, you will:

* Substantiate your company's expertise, message, and brand.
* Enrich your company's relationships with its critical stakeholders, including key customers and prospects, partners, opinion leaders, the media, and internal audiences.
* Improve visibility and stature of your C-suite executives and your whole public-facing leadership team.
* Influence the industry conversation at all levels—and give you the opportunity to become known for key parts of it!

Get this right, and your company will generate the following outcomes and results:

* Reputation
* Differentiation
* Risk reduction
* Client relationships
* Brand association
* Long-term revenue
* Environment impact
* Economic development
* New opportunities
* Perception shifting
* PR and media exposure

* Client education
* Network growth
* Building trust
* Innovation

Maximize your return on the marketing investments you're already making in sending your C-level executives, senior leadership team, and marketing/sales executives to conferences and events . . . so that you can generate MORE leads, BETTER prospects, and BIGGER sales.

To this end, we always recommend our corporate clients develop a "Speaker Scorecard" for each event, which normally would include whatever metrics are important to advance your goals. For example:

Event: _____

Date: _____

Executives presenting: _____

Topic: _____

Attendance: _____

Number of leads: _____

Number of appointments: _____

Revenue generated: $ _____

Number of opportunities: _____

Number of sales: _____

Number of strategic partnerships/connections: _____

Projected economic impact of partnerships: $_____

Observations of content, pace, and impact of presentation: _____

_____

_____

Observations of audience response to calls to action: _____

_____

_____

Recommended ways to improve for next event (pre-, during, and post-):

_____

_____

_____

Activation, socialization, and PR impact of speaking at this event (pre-, during, and post-): _____

_____

_____

_____

Overall evaluation of this audience/event/opportunity for next year:

_____

_____

_____

_____

For a downloadable copy of this "Speaker Scorecard," visit www.doit marketing.com/speak.

DO IT! SUCCESS STRATEGY: SPEAKING SUCCESS AFTER THE C-SUITE

BY JEFFREY HAYZLETT, CPAE

As C-suite leaders, we're entrusted to deliver results, increase the bottom line, and make shareholders happy. Whether you're a CMO, a CFO, or a CTO, the pressure to deliver is endless and it can be crushing at times. There's very little room for error and the stakes are always high.

The average tenure of a CMO is the lowest of all C-suite titles, at an average of 4.1 years, according to analysis from the Korn Ferry Institute. Within the consumer industry, CMOs last a little over three years. Overall, C-suite roles are fleeting and don't necessarily provide a long shelf life or tenure. Therefore, it is always a smart move to explore other avenues as your next career move—especially public speaking.

During my tenure as a Fortune 100 CMO, my position offered me a number of opportunities to branch out, which I probably wouldn't have had at other jobs. As a CMO, my main role was to be the front

(continues)

person for the brand, an amplification of that brand for customers, vendors, and shareholders alike. When you're a member of the C-suite, one your biggest responsibilities involves communicating the values of your brand every single day. After all, a brand is nothing but a promise delivered and I had to communicate those promises across all platforms and at all levels.

Another part of my job involved speaking to a number of different groups—on TV and onstage. I was on the BBC in the UK or on ABC Australia talking about the company and the brand. That experience helped me hone my skills as a speaker, making it the next logical step in my career. I saw speaking as an extension of my current CMO role, but on a different stage. Take away the cameras and there's still a stage and an audience to impress. I had the luxury of polishing those skills prior to my C-suite-level position as a member of the National Speakers Association (NSA), so for me, it was pretty easy to figure out where I'd be going next.

If you're thinking about becoming a speaker, let me give you a little tip—this is not something you can make up as you go along. The famous adage "fake it until you make it" will get you in a lot of trouble. People can spot a phony, or worse, a wannabe, from miles away, and just like that, your credibility becomes nonexistent. If you're serious about becoming a speaker, you have to actually be good at it, and in order to be good at it, you must practice! Whether you practice in front of a mirror using a hairbrush as a microphone, or you read your speech to your family a hundred times, you have to practice. Don't wing it, don't fake it. Ever!

So, the best advice I can give any C-suite leader looking to become a speaker in the next stage of their career is this: Ask yourself where you want your journey to take you. Whatever that is, know there will be plenty of twists, turns, stops, and restarts along the way. One thing's for sure—your endpoint will not be the same one you thought of when you began the journey. Have a plan and execute the plan to the best of your abilities. That's how you succeed after life in the C-suite!

69 THE SHAME OF SUCCESS

If you'd like to do better in your speaking-driven business . . . this one is for you.

If you're **down in the dumps**—no money, no clients, no prospects, no hope . . . this one is for you.

If you're **doing great**—and not sure exactly why or how long this "lucky streak" will last— this one is DEFINITELY for you . . .

There's a dirty word in business, especially among top speakers, executives, and entrepreneurs who feel that they should serve as shining examples of personal success and professional prosperity.

That word is shame.

 **@dnewman**

It's easy to feel shame when your business is doing poorly.
I'm not saying that it's RIGHT—but it sure is easy.

And yes, it's painful, negative, and unpleasant to feel shame. But perhaps there's an upside to that because it makes you feel uncomfortable to feel unsuccessful. At least THAT part makes sense.

There's another kind of shame that is more pernicious, dangerous, and much more common than you might think.

It's the shame of success.

It's when you juuuuust start to break through . . . when your speaking-driven business juuuuust starts to take off . . . when the money juuuuust starts to flow abundantly.

You're not only paying your bills, you're paying off debt (credit cards, home equity line, etc.), you're building up your savings, your rainy-day fund is healthy, you're paying yourself regularly, you are even (gasp!) putting away some nice money for retirement and/or your kids' college fund.

Then it hits you . . . the shame of success. It's a little voice in your head. You know what I'm talking about. I'll bet you even know what it's saying to you. It's saying things like:

* This won't last—it's just a lucky streak . . .
* You're one step away from being broke again . . .
* Don't count your eggs before they hatch . . .
* You're not that good . . .
* You're not that smart . . .
* You can't even handle this much client work . . .
* You're going to blow through all this cash and be back at square one . . .
* Your clients will find you out . . .
* Your friends won't like your new level of success . . .
* Better not tell anyone about this success, they'll be jealous . . .
* They'll think you're lying . . .
* They'll think you're bragging . . .
* They'll feel bad that they're not doing as well as you . . .

And on, and on, and on.

Please . . . stop the madness. Kill that voice.

Catch yourself every time you hear it and tell it to go take a hike. Refocus. Recenter.

@dnewman

Remember once and for all that there is no shame in your success.

If you have REAL friends, they'll celebrate with you. If you have friends who don't . . . guess what? They're not your real friends.

If misery loves company, it has company enough.

And it's time you quit that company.

You know who REALLY loves company?

* ✸ Passion loves company.
* ✸ Achievers love company.
* ✸ Winners love company.
* ✸ Success loves company.

There are already way too many forces working against you that make you feel weak, unworthy, and unsuccessful . . . Do NOT be one of them!

* ✸ FACT: You TOTALLY deserve to be successful.
* ✸ FACT: This is ABSOLUTELY your time to crush it.
* ✸ FACT: YOU ROCK so hard, you don't even know it.
* ✸ FACT: You are insanely GREAT.

Bottom line: You ARE fabulously successful—so KEEP GOING!!!

70 STOP THE MARKETING MONKEY WORK

If you feel overwhelmed with the hundred market-

ing jobs you've assigned yourself, you're exhausted, and you're tired of feeling like you're spinning your wheels but getting nowhere, you are hereby getting my official permission to STOP.

Focus on the kinds of marketing activities you find easy, effortless, and enjoyable. If you like to write, use writing strategies. If you hate to write, then of course you'll find blogging, article marketing, and writing an email newsletter painful, hard, and unpleasant. Guess what? We tend NOT to do things that we find painful, hard, and unpleasant so you're going to quit.

One of my favorite marketing mantras is . . .

 @dnewman

It's amazing the results you do not get from the marketing you do not DO.

If you love to speak, use speaking strategies. Obviously, you wouldn't have picked up this book if you hated speaking, but . . . consider other ways to "speak as a marketing strategy." You could host your own podcast just like I host *The Speaking Show* (TheSpeakingShow.com—come check it out) or be a guest on other experts' podcasts that reach your same target market. Doing Facebook Live or other livestreaming is a speaking strategy.

Recording YouTube videos and building an audience there is a speaking strategy. Lead-generating speaking in front of highly targeted groups is obviously a speaking strategy. Doing a regular series of webinars is a speaking strategy.

On the other hand, if you're geeky and you love technology, use technology strategies. Fiddle around with search engine optimization. Install a bot on your website to capture leads. Use a series of juicy lead magnets, downloads, or videos to walk prospects through an online funnel where you offer value and invite engagement. Play with the latest and greatest social media platform to see how you can use it to both serve your prospects and help them buy from you.

Some other folks don't like to write, might not want to be on camera all the time, don't like tech, but, oh boy—do they ever love meeting new people, shaking hands, and kissing babies. If you love in-person strategies, then use in-person strategies. Network, meet new people, invite centers of influence to breakfast, lunch, or coffee. Use networking and referral strategies to connect with people, be helpful to them, and help them build their business as they help you build yours.

This isn't rocket science: If you love writing, write. If you love speaking, speak. If you love tech, do the tech. If you love people, go meet some.

The reason your marketing needs to be *easy, effortless,* and *enjoyable* is simple: It's also the only marketing that will be EFFECTIVE because you're much more likely to implement it. Even on the days you might not feel like doing so.

 @dnewman

What will you do every single day, rain or shine, happy or sad, feel like it or not, to move your business forward?

71 THE SPEAKER PROFIT FORMULA

This is the great formula that will help you crack

the code on your speaking success. This is the proven seven-step system to help you go from initial contact to signed contract as a paid professional speaker. Let's take a closer look at this magic formula on this grid:

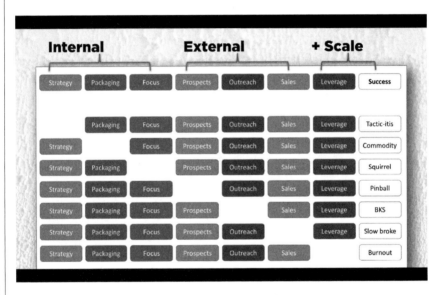

Internal			External			+ Scale	
Strategy	Packaging	Focus	Prospects	Outreach	Sales	Leverage	Success
	Packaging	Focus	Prospects	Outreach	Sales	Leverage	Tactic-itis
Strategy		Focus	Prospects	Outreach	Sales	Leverage	Commodity
Strategy	Packaging		Prospects	Outreach	Sales	Leverage	Squirrel
Strategy	Packaging	Focus		Outreach	Sales	Leverage	Pinball
Strategy	Packaging	Focus	Prospects		Sales	Leverage	BKS
Strategy	Packaging	Focus	Prospects	Outreach		Leverage	Slow broke
Strategy	Packaging	Focus	Prospects	Outreach	Sales		Burnout

The cool thing with this model is I could sit down with you over a cup of coffee, we'd have a five-minute conversation about your speaking business, and I could tell exactly which piece (or which pieces) are missing for YOU in your particular speaking business.

Let's go down the list and we'll see how you do. (Bring your own coffee for this time!)

First one is no Strategy. No strategy obviously leads to tactic–itis. Trying tactic after tactic after tactic with no real strategy and no real results. Or—even worse—random tactics that lead to random results!

Having no Packaging leads to the commodity problem. As a commodity, you're a same-o lame-o speaker, meaning you look like, sound like, act like everybody else.

Having no Focus means that you're a squirrel. You're suffering from entrepreneurial Attention Deficit Disorder (ADD). You suffer from "SOS" (shiny-object syndrome) and you're bouncing all over the map with no focus. Easily pulled off task with distractions disguised as opportunities, you never seem to get any traction on your marketing, your sales, or your big projects.

If you don't have a Prospecting game plan, you'll find yourself pinballing all over the place. Bouncing from this group to that industry, to this niche, to over here, over there. You never know where your next new lead is coming from. As far as you know, all of your prospects fall into your lap out of the blue because it's totally random and totally reactive.

With no Outreach, you suffer from best-kept-secret syndrome. Obviously, if you don't consistently and powerfully reach out and connect to the buyers in your marketplace, you ARE going to be the best-kept secret in your niche and in your industry; and no one is going to know your name.

If you don't have a Sales mind-set and skill set, you're going to be slowly going broke. This is what I was doing in the first three years of my speaking business. I had no sales process, no sales mind-set, no sales skills—and I was dipping into savings and rapidly sliding into what ultimately became $40,000 of credit card debt. Maybe you're withdrawing money from your IRA or your pension or your retirement but it's not going well. You're cash flow negative.

Then the final challenge is no Leverage. No leverage means that you're on the hamster wheel and you're going from gig to gig to gig— and even if that's working for you, you're not able to sustain success and you're not able to keep your pipeline or bank account full because you're on the revenue roller coaster. Some months you're up, some months you're down. And you also don't have any way of generating revenue that is NOT tied to your personal time, attention, and presence. Lack of leverage ultimately causes burnout.

72 THE NEW RULES FOR EXPERTS WHO SPEAK

1. **Think beyond the keynote.** What other formats can you deliver your expertise in? Think in terms of onstage interviews, interactive discussions, group masterminding, and getting the audience to connect and tap into each other and hybrid "keynote-seminar-workshop" formats. Because the era of the talking head, one-way data dump is over. Meeting planners and conference producers and association executives today want more inter-activity, more hands-on, more engagement, more dialogue, and more experiential programs. You really have to think beyond the keynote.

2. **You don't want to be asked to do it again.** If you keep getting asked back, to do it again, do it again, do it again, this causes the gig-to-gig hamster wheel. Think about transactions versus transformations. A one-time speech is transactional. What audiences and clients and buyers really want is transformation. After you're done speaking, you don't want them to say, "Hey, come do it again." You want them to say, "This was awe-some—what's next? How can we get more of this? What can you offer to help us go deeper?" Use the first program to open the door to lots of other work that your clients and audiences want and need.

3. **Professional Speaker is a skill set—not a job description.** I want you to focus on all possible distribution methods for your expertise. In fact, I would even redefine what you're doing: You're not a professional speaker, you're a professional thinker and professional problem solver. Let your clients connect what they want and need with how they want to buy you. Don't be married to any particular distribution method. Maybe it's a speech. But you know what? Maybe it's a year-long professional develop-ment program. Maybe it's buying ten thousand copies of your book.

Maybe it's doing executive coaching with their top leadership team. Don't restrict yourself to just speaking, speaking, speaking.

4. Training is the most popular mode of delivery for live events. What can YOU do to supplement and complement your speaking with training? It could be live training, video training, on-site training, training assessments and tools, e-learning and online courses, or even "train the trainer" certifications or licensing your intellectual property for other speakers and consultants to use or for your client companies to distribute in-house.

5. Consider the Golden Triangle—This is what can fuel your entire thought-leadership business. It's such a powerful concept, it deserves a deeper dive.

Let's do that right now . . .

73 THE GOLDEN TRIANGLE

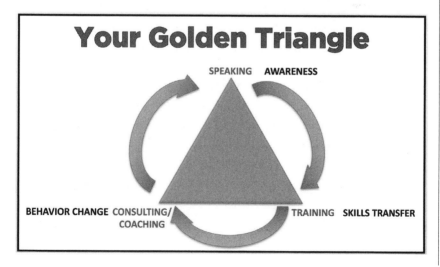

Your Golden Triangle

SPEAKING AWARENESS

BEHAVIOR CHANGE CONSULTING/ COACHING

TRAINING SKILLS TRANSFER

The Golden Triangle starts out with **Speaking**. The only thing speaking is ever going to do (no matter how great a speaker you are) is raise **awareness**.

You do a good job there, they're going to say, "Hey, David, what's next? What else can we do? How else can we go deeper?" Then they're going to buy your **Training** solutions because training is where **skills transfer** happens.

You do a good job with that and they're going to want to go even deeper with you on a long-term, sustainable basis and that's where your **Consulting and Coaching** comes in because that's where you get true **behavior change**.

Now, you can keep going around this Golden Triangle. You do a great job with the speech, now they want training. You do a great job with the training, now they want long-term consulting or coaching and now they might start to refer and recommend you to other regions, other departments, other business units, or other companies.

In a large corporation, for example, they might hand you off from business unit to business unit to business unit. You can keep going around this Golden Triangle over and over and over again where speaking leads to training leads to consulting and coaching leads to more speaking for a different group as you start to penetrate that company and they start to pass you around like candy to the tune of possibly hundreds of thousands of dollars over a multiyear period.

This can be enormously profitable with only a small handful of clients. Start working on your Golden Triangle business model and watch your revenues take off!

74 HOW TO CRUSH IT THIS YEAR AND EVERY YEAR

If you want to make the next twelve months more successful, more profitable, and more productive than the last twelve months, these ten strategies are for you.

By the way, this list isn't just for a new calendar year—you can revisit this list at any time and create a real turning point in your business if you're willing to reboot, reinvigorate, and reimagine your business success.

1. **List the three most important objectives for your business** over the next year. These should be critical big-picture accomplishments that will lead to profits and future achievement.

2. **For each objective listed above,** identify your responsibility in achieving the objective. WHAT will you do? HOW will you do it? WHEN will you do it?

3. **Be crystal clear** in separating strategies (how and why items) from tactics (what and when items) and use "verb-noun-date" format to create specific action steps and put them on your calendar.

4. **Don't think of the year as a whole.** Break it down to monthly metrics and put quarterly goal-planning reviews on your calendar so you can adjust the dials on your plan, measure results, and take a strategic look at your marketing, sales, and business development activities every ninety days while keeping a close eye on results (profits, clients, projects, revenue) every thirty days.

5. Don't go it alone. Remember, lone wolves starve to death. Think of partners, allies, referral sources, influencers, and joint venture partners who can help you leapfrog over obstacles and who are a great supplement and complement to your own products and services. Contact them and build (or grow) your relationship with them so you can collaborate more closely—starting right now.

6. Write down a list of professional development goals for the next twelve months. What do you want to learn, do, or become as a business owner? Go to conferences? Gain additional certifications or professional designations? Speak more? Get more articles published? Be specific and put these activities on your calendar so you make sure they happen.

7. Write down a list of personal goals for the next twelve months. What do you want to accomplish for yourself and how would you like to grow personally? Spend more time with your partner? Stay connected with your kids as they grow up and/or pursue their college or post-college adventures? Dig deeper into a special hobby or sport? Drop ten pounds? Run a 5K? More golf? More vacation time? Where? When? With whom? Map it out to make it happen!

8. Don't get distracted. Shiny object syndrome has a powerful pull on most entrepreneurs and business owners. Stay focused on the big-picture goals you set in Step 1 above—and then relentlessly ask yourself for every new idea, initiative, or project, "Does this support one of my three goals? If so, how?" And don't let yourself off the hook as easily as you might have done in the past. If it's a no, it's a no. Metaphorically speaking, stop opening up hot dog stands in the parking lot and redouble your efforts to make your gourmet restaurant thrive!

9. Live out of your calendar, not your inbox. Plan your day—what MUST get done and WHEN? Chunk your day down into blocks and assign specific tasks to those blocks—phone calls, emails, client tasks, whatever it is YOU want to do that will move you closer to your GOALS. Keep that calendar under your nose. All day. Make it your default screen. Hide, minimize, or (gasp!) close your email until "check email" pops up on your calendar.

10. **Breathe. Relax. You've got this.** Any time you're creating an inflection point in your business, it can be scary. You're letting go of the old—letting go of what no longer works or what no longer serves you well. And you're embracing the new—the untried, the uncomfortable, perhaps even what seems risky. But the biggest risks of all are stagnation, arrogance, or complacency. Remember: A bend in the road is never a dead end . . . unless you fail to turn.

75 THE FOUR LEVELS OF MARKETING

When it comes to marketing, there are four things

that you need to focus on—four levels, if you will.

The four levels of marketing are:

1. Strategy
2. Tactics
3. Initiatives
4. Action steps

When you go to a conference, when you ask your mastermind group for help, even when you start searching the web for answers and resources to grow your business, the **number one source of overwhelm** is when you've heard a whole bunch of strategies, a whole bunch of tactics, a whole bunch of initiatives, a whole bunch of action steps, and you don't know the difference.

There are three reasons why this short-circuits your brain:

1. You can't do them all.

2. You can't even prioritize or figure out how to start to think about them.
3. You can't distinguish which is which and why or how it might work for your particular business.

A **strategy** is a big-picture area of your business. It could be a marketing-focused strategy. It could be a sales-focused strategy. It could be a financial strategy.

Let's say you come across someone who tells you Twitter is an amazing marketing platform and you're really missing out if your business is not on Twitter. He's using it and it fits his business beautifully, and you respect this person and you admire his successful business.

And now you're thinking, "Oh man, it's all about Twitter, Twitter, Twitter."

"If this guy built his business on Twitter, I can probably build my business on Twitter."

Well, let's back up and analyze that as far as the four levels of marketing.

Internet marketing is the **strategy**. In other words, internet marketing is the big giant umbrella over Twitter.

The **tactic** under that would be **social media**. There's a lot going on via the internet, folks, that's not social media.

For example, search engine optimization, your website, the structure of your web presence, blogging, email marketing, dozens of internet marketing strategies. Social media happens to be one bucket under that, so social media is the tactic.

An **initiative** would be: **"I'm going to start using Twitter."**

This is level three now. I'm going to start using Twitter. I'm going to start understanding it. I might read a book. I might go to some websites. I'm going to grab a copy of *Twitter 101* or *Using Twitter for Business*, all those fabulous resources that are out there for free.

Now, the **action step**—here's level four, the action step always takes the form of **verb, noun, date**.

* Set up my Twitter account by Wednesday.
* Load my first thirty tweets in Hootsuite by Friday.
* Find a hundred influential people to follow in my industry by next Monday.

Those are action steps.

And the action step can also go on your calendar.

So it really takes it down to: "What are you doing **today**?" What's on your priority to-do list **today**?

Your to-do list could be fifty things, but what are **your top three most important things** that you need to do based on the **strategies** you've selected, based on the **tactics** that you've chosen, based on the **initiatives** that you've designed—what are the **action steps** to put on your calendar and get it done?

So let's follow this through with a complete example—let's say you're in the insurance business.

You're selling into the insurance marketplace, insurance companies and insurance agents, general agents, insurance associations, insurance publications, and you're looking to become a dominant resource in that world.

Your **action step** would be: "I want to follow three hundred insurance industry folks on Twitter by March 1."

Does that fit into an **initiative**? Yes. The initiative is to aggressively grow my Twitter following targeted to the insurance industry.

Does that fit into a **tactic**? Yes, it does. It fits into the social media set of tactics.

Does that fall under a **strategy** that you decided to use? Yes, it falls under your internet marketing strategy.

So right there, just unpacking those four levels, **you've gotten some insights through which you can start to filter and sort** all of your old ideas, old notes, all of those conference sessions that you may have gone to, all of those tactics and tools and light-bulb moments, all those nuggets and sound bites that you may have swirling around in your head or on your "someday, maybe" list.

If you start to sort them in to these four levels—**strategy, tactic, initiative,** and **action step**—you'll get a much clearer blueprint for ALL your marketing going forward this month, next month, and next year.

76 SEVEN THINGS SMART SPEAKERS DO DAILY

Here are the top seven things that smart speakers,

consultants, and experts must do every single day:

1. **Revisit your goals, milestones, and metrics** for the day, week, month, and quarter (financial, marketing, sales, operations).
   Ramifications if not done daily—you lose sight of the big picture and get pulled off your game by distractions, trivia, and grunt work.

2. **Put new prospects on your radar** via strategic outreach . . .
   Ramifications if not done daily—your sales and marketing start to slip, and you suffer from the feast-or-famine revenue roller coaster.

3. **Thank your team**—whether in-house, outsourced, full-time, or virtual . . .
   Ramifications if not done daily—your team loses their motivation, momentum, and mojo. Once that's gone, they're halfway out the door.

4. **Offer value**—in terms of content, your blog, a video, a resource, a referral, a favor, a gift . . .
   Ramifications if not done daily—you become just more marketing noise and clients and prospects tune you out and see you as a peddler, not a partner.

5. **Invite engagement**—online, offline, in-person, by phone or Skype; ask and answer questions, solicit feedback, invite comments, send a survey . . .
   Ramifications if not done daily—your business becomes isolated as you talk AT your prospects and clients rather than talk WITH them.

6. Recharge your batteries—just like the airlines say, "secure your own mask before assisting others" . . .

Ramifications if not done daily—entrepreneurial burnout, stress, drinking, drugs, and divorce. Don't laugh—you could be next.

7. Be gracious and grateful—take a moment to appreciate what you have, what you've built, and who you get to serve each day . . .

Ramifications if not done daily—instead of becoming more and more fulfilling, your business success becomes a trap, a race, and a never-ending contest that you can never win. Stop and smell the coffee!

77 TEN QUESTIONS TO SPARK YOUR SUCCESS

1. There's no good time. Now is the time. What are you waiting for?

2. Put out your best material. For free. Do you want to be SHARED or SCARED?

3. YOU may be your biggest obstacle. What would happen if you got out of the way?

4. Stop STARTING things and get more into DOING. What can you do today—right now?

5. A few may wish to see you fail. A lot more are rooting for your success. Where is your attention?

6.   **Forget the word *vision*.** Better: What do you SEE in your future?

7.   **You're aiming too low.** How can you elevate your sights, your fees, and your value?

8.   **Stop blaming others. It's ALL your fault.** Move on—what's next?

9.   **It's not what you think it is. And it's bigger than you think it is.** Why not embrace that?

10.   **There are no silver bullets, secret sauces, or magic beans.** Now, what's your plan?

CONTINUE THE JOURNEY

Thank you for reading all the way to the end.

Of course, every ending is simply the beginning of something new and it's no different with this book.

To extend your learning, doing, and results, here are some resources, tools, and experiences to help you speak more profitably.

THE SPEAKER PROFIT FORMULA® MENTORING PROGRAM

Intensive and personalized mentoring for executives and entrepreneurs who want to position themselves as thought leaders and win more clients, more easily, and more often using the power of paid professional speaking. Details at SpeakerProfitFormula.com.

THE SPEAKER PROFIT FORMULA® WORKSHOP

Bring the marketing, sales, branding, and lead generation power of speaking to your entire team. This experiential hands-on workshop is always customized to your exact situation, industry, and goals and we share an intensive two-day experience crafting your plan for global domination to win more stages and win more business.

THE SPEAKER VIDEO SUMMIT

For executive and entrepreneurial speakers who want to create a top-notch speaker video. Includes pre-event preparation, evaluating your practice videos, and personal feedback and coaching on both content and delivery. Then we convene for two days in a beautiful theater setting for a three-camera HD video shoot. You get a fully edited video primer, expert interview, testimonials, action photos, all raw footage and the master edit file to integrate video assets you may already have.

Details at SpeakerVideoSummit.com.

KEYNOTES THAT CONVERT

Anyone can teach presentation skills or how to craft a good speech. But not everyone can teach you how to craft a killer keynote that reliably converts into more prospects, leads, and sales. Over the course of an intense two-day seminar in a boardroom setting, you'll get everything you need to outline, build, and deliver a compelling keynote that is also your best marketing tool for your company's services, products, and pro-grams—without the usual "selling from the stage" nonsense and without shortchanging your audience in any way. In fact, after this seminar, you'll come to realize that crafting a "great keynote" IS a keynote that converts into results—for you, your company, and your audience!

Details at KeynotesThatConvert.com.

THE SPEAKING SHOW PODCAST

A Top 50 business podcast on iTunes, *The Speaking Show* is an interview-based podcast focused on a core audience of speakers, consul-tants, and thought-leading executives and entrepreneurs (good-looking folks like YOU) who want instant-action strategies, advice, and insights to grow your speaking-driven business.

Tune in and subscribe at TheSpeakingShow.com.

FREE SPEAKER TRAINING AND MASTER CLASSES

Visit doitmarketing.com/webinar to get our latest web training for experts who want to speak more profitably.

CLAIM YOUR FREE CONFIDENTIAL SPEAKER STRATEGY SESSION

We like working with smart, ambitious people who want to speak more, earn more, and become authorities in their fields. We'll take a deep-dive diagnostic look at your positioning, packaging, marketing, prospecting, outreach, sales, and overall mix of strategies, tactics, and tools to help you see exactly what's working, what's not, and how to fix it (without all the marketing monkey work you hate). Sessions always fill quickly every month. Visit doitmarketing.com/call.

DO IT! MARKETING® MANIFESTO

Bad news: Marketing for the sake of marketing is broken. Kaput. Finished. Smart marketing is all about helping you generate MORE leads, BETTER prospects, and BIGGER sales. Good news: That also happens to be the purpose of this cheeky, powerful little manifesto you're about to read. Visit doitmarketing.com/manifesto.

ACKNOWLEDGMENTS

First, the personal: Thank you to my best friend and marriage partner of thirty-five years, Vanessa Christman, who gets a ton of credit for sticking with me through thick and thin. Without you, none of this would be any fun at all. You're my #1 consigliere, consultant, travel partner, and coconspirator of awesomeness.

My two amazing kids, Becca and Charlie, were both living at home when *Do It! Marketing* came out, and now, they're both successfully launched adults with real jobs, cars, apartments, and cats. Oh, and I now have two grandcats—so thank you to Agnes and Rayna.

Our black Lab, Woofie the Wonder Dog, is always in our hearts, and her website delights her millions of fans at WheresWoofie.com. We love you, Woofs!

Next, the professional: I'm grateful to my amazing team at Do It! Marketing. I love working with you and appreciate you more than you know. There's no better team of rebels, rock stars, and revolutionaries. Thank you for being of profound service to our clients every single day.

Thank you to the more than eight hundred speakers, consultants, entrepreneurs, and executives whom I've had the privilege to work with individually, in our Speaker Profit Formula® mentoring program, in our Keynotes That Convert seminars, in our Persuasion Architecture® master classes, in our corporate keynotes and on-site workshops, and through our Platinum mastermind programs. YOU are both the proving ground for these ideas, and the successful result of all the hard work you put in to operationalize these strategies, tactics, and tools.

I'm continually humbled and grateful for your confidence, your business, your friendship, and the credit that you bring to our work by DOING

IT consistently, smartly, and bravely. You are the embodiment of my mantra: "Only action creates results." Thank you for the privilege of working alongside you as you create your next level of success.

I'm also grateful to the super-talented Chris Murray, whose editing skill, patience, and intuitive brilliance shaped this book into what you're holding in your hands right now. Chris took a primordial soup of raw content and ideas to extract the gems, make them shine, and collate, curate, sequence, and improve them at every step of the process. Chris is the best in the business. When you write your next book, you NEED this guy. Expensive and worth it. Get on his waiting list by emailing chris@chrismurrayeditor.com.

Big thanks to my literary agent, Michael Snell. Ellen Kadin, formerly at AMACOM, was instrumental to the success of my first book, *Do It! Marketing*, which made this second book possible.

Thank you to Sara Kendrick, Tim Burgard, Hiram Centeno, Sicily Axton, Leigh Grossman, and the whole team at HarperCollins.

Thank you to four very special people who helped me at every point in my entrepreneurial journey, including the good, the bad, and the ugly: in mind (Terry Fisher), in body (Nick Odorisio), in spirit (Scott Simons), and in career (Ford R. Myers).

Thank you to my expert contributors: Jay Baer, Corey Perlman, Mark Levy, Sam Richter, Dan Janal, Scott McKain, Ed Rigsbee, David Siteman Garland, Mark Hunter, Henry DeVries, Bill Cates, Jeffrey Hayzlett, Art Sobczak, Debbie Allen, Michael Goldberg, Karyn Greenstreet. You are each superheroes in your own realm, and I hugely appreciate your generosity of expertise.

And my best and last thank you has to go to *YOU*—for buying this book, for reading it, and for applying its strategies, tactics, and tools to build your speaker brand, grow your company, and expand your career as an expert who speaks professionally.

ACKNOWLEDGMENTS

ABOUT THE AUTHOR

David Newman, CSP is a nationally acclaimed marketing expert who works with C-suite leaders, executives, and entrepreneurs who want to speak more profitably and unleash the power of speaking as the ultimate marketing strategy, personal brand builder, and 1-to-many sales platform.

David is the author of the #1 business bestseller *Do It! Marketing* and he's the creator of the Speaker Profit Formula® flagship mentoring program with more than eight hundred successful graduates. David is the host of the iTunes Top 50 business podcast *The Speaking Show*.

David has been working at the intersection of marketing, technology, and professional services since 1992. His clients and audiences include Accenture, KPMG, Oracle, IBM, Microsoft, PriceWaterhouseCoopers, and forty-four of the Fortune 500.

He is an experienced professional services marketer, professional speaker, and strategic business coach. David has presented for over six hundred groups, including state and national associations, nonprofit organizations, and companies of every size.

In 2017, David was inducted into the National Speakers Association's prestigious Million Dollar Speakers Group and he is a Benefactor Member of NSA.

David has been featured and quoted in the *New York Times*, *Investor's Business Daily*, *Forbes*, *MSN*, *StartupNation*, *FastCompany.com*, *Sales & Marketing Management*, *Selling Power*, *Thrive Global*, CNBC, and *Entrepreneur* magazine.

David is married to the number one most amazing woman on the planet, launched two great kids into the world disguised as small adults, and has the world's sweetest Labrador retriever named Woofie (who has her own website at www.WheresWoofie.com). Get your free companion trainings, templates, and tools (plus some cool bonuses) at doitmarketing.com/speaking.

INDEX